NORTHERN CALIFORNIA NATURE GUIDE

Erin McCloskey

with contributions from Andy Bezener,
Krista Kagume & Linda Kershaw

LONE PINE

Lone Pine Publishing International

Distributed by Lone Pine Publishing
1808 B Street NW, Suite 140
Auburn, WA, USA 98001

Website: www.lonepinepublishing.com

Publisher's Cataloging-In-Publication Data
(Prepared by The Donohue Group, Inc.)

McCloskey, Erin, 1970–
   Northern California nature guide / Erin McCloskey.

   p. : col. ill., col. maps ; cm.

   Includes bibliographical references and index.
   ISBN-13: 978-976-8200-44-0
   ISBN-10: 976-8200-44-8

1. Natural history—California, Northern—Guidebooks. 2. California, Northern—Guidebooks. I. Title.

QH105.C2 M33 2008
508.7/94

Cover Illustrations: Ted Nordhagen, Gary Ross, Ian Sheldon
Illustrations: Frank Burman, Ivan Droujinin, Kindrie Grove, Linda Kershaw, Ted Nordhagen, George Penetrante, Gary Ross, Ian Sheldon
A complete list of illustration credits appears on p. 4.

Disclaimer: This guide is not intended to be a "how to" reference guide for food or medicinal uses of plants. We do not recommend experimentation by readers, and we caution that a number of plants in Northern California , including some used traditionally as medicines, are poisonous and harmful.

PC: P15

TABLE OF CONTENTS

ILLUSTRATION CREDITS

Frank Burman: 153a, 153b, 154, 156c, 156d, 157, 158, 159, 160, 162, 163a, 163c, 167b, 167c, 168b, 168c, 170c, 170d, 171b, 171c, 172a, 173a, 173b, 173c, 175b, 175c, 178b, 179a, 179b, 180b, 180c, 181a, 181c, 182a, 182c, 183, 184, 185a, 185c, 186, 187, 188b, 188c, 189c, 190e, 191, 192, 193c, 194a, 194c, 195a, 195c, 196a, 197b, 197c, 198a

Ivan Droujinin: 117a, 117b, 121a, 122a, 124b, 124c, 150c

Kindrie Grove: 73a

Linda Kershaw: 175a

Ted Nordhagen: 83c, 89c, 91b, 91c, 92a, 92b, 96a, 97c, 100b, 101, 102a, 102c, 103a, 104a, 105a, 105c, 106, 107, 108, 109b, 109c, 110c, 111c, 112b, 113c, 114b, 115

George Penetrante: 129b, 129c, 130b

Gary Ross: 48, 49, 50, 51, 52, 53, 58b, 59b, 60, 61, 62, 63, 64, 65, 66, 67, 68, 69, 70, 71, 72, 73b, 73c, 74, 77, 78, 79, 80, 81, 82, 83a, 83b, 84, 85, 86, 87, 88, 89a, 89b, 90, 91a, 92c, 93, 94, 95, 96b, 96c, 97a, 97b, 98, 99, 100a, 100c, 102b, 103b, 103c, 104b, 104c, 105b, 109a, 110a, 110b, 111a, 111b, 112a, 112c, 113a, 113b, 114a, 114c, 117c, 118, 119, 120, 121c, 123, 124a, 125

Ian Sheldon: 54, 55, 56, 57, 58a, 59a, 121b, 122b, 127, 128, 129a, 130a, 133, 134, 135, 136, 137, 138, 139, 140, 141, 142, 143, 144, 145, 146, 147, 148, 149, 150a, 150b, 153c, 153d, 155, 156a, 156b, 161, 163b, 166, 167a, 167d, 167e, 168a, 169, 170a, 170b, 171a, 172b, 172c, 173d, 173e, 174, 178a, 178c, 179c, 180a, 181b, 182b, 185b, 188a, 189a, 189b, 190a, 190b, 190c, 190d, 193a, 193b, 194b, 195b, 196b, 196c, 197a, 198b, 198c, 199

ACKNOWLEDGMENTS

The publisher and author thank Tamara Eder and Krista Kagume for their previous work on the mammals and birds research and all the authors of former Lone Pine texts who have created such a great library of background information. Thanks to Andy Bezener and Linda Kershaw for their work on the first of this nature guide series, the *Rocky Mountain Nature Guide*.

Special thanks to the following people for their assistance in the development of the species lists: Ian Sheldon (author and illustrator of *Seashore Guide of Northern California* and *Bugs of Northern California*), Maddalena Bearzi, PhD (president and co-founder of the Ocean Conservation Society), Dawn Hayes (education and outreach coordinator for the National Oceanic and Atmospheric Administration), Gary M. Langham (director of bird conservation, Audubon California), John Malpas (Calflora) and Mike Landram (silviculture group leader, US Forest Service).

MAMMALS

Bighorn Sheep
p. 48

Pronghorn
p. 48

Elk
p. 49

Mule Deer
p. 49

Feral Horse
p. 50

Feral Pig
p. 50

Mountain Lion
p. 51

Bobcat
p. 51

American Black Bear
p. 52

Coyote
p. 52

Gray Fox
p. 53

Kit Fox
p. 53

Red Fox
p. 53

Gray Whale
p. 54

Minke Whale
p. 54

Fin Whale
p. 55

Humpback Whale
p. 55

Orca
p. 56

Bottlenose Dolphin
p. 56

Short-beaked Common
Dolphin, p. 57

Risso's Dolphin
p. 57

Northern Elephant Seal
p. 58

Harbor Seal
p. 58

California Sea-lion
p. 59

Sea Otter
p. 59

Northern River Otter
p. 60

Fisher
p. 60

American Marten
p. 60

Short-tailed Weasel
p. 61

Long-tailed Weasel
p. 61

American Mink
p. 61

Wolverine
p. 62

Badger
p. 62

Striped Skunk
p. 62

Western Spotted Skunk
p. 63

Ringtail
p. 63

Raccoon
p. 63

Porcupine
p. 64

Mountain Beaver
p. 64

Beaver
p. 64

Common Muskrat
p. 65

Bushy-tailed Woodrat
p. 65

Deer Mouse
p. 65

California Vole
p. 66

California Kangaroo Rat
p. 66

Botta's Pocket Gopher
p. 66

California Ground Squirrel
p. 67

Yellow-bellied Marmot
p. 67

Yellow-pine Chipmunk
p. 67

Gray Western Squirrel
p. 68

Northern Flying Squirrel
p. 68

Snowshoe Hare
p. 68

Black-tailed Jackrabbit
p. 69

Pygmy Rabbit
p. 69

Brush Rabbit
p. 69

Mountain Cottontail
p. 70

Pika
p. 70

Brazilian Free-tailed Bat
p. 70

Western Mastiff Bat
p. 71

Little Brown Bat
p. 71

Hoary Bat
p. 71

MAMMALS

Western Pipistrelle
p. 72

Silver-haired Bat
p. 72

Big Brown Bat
p. 72

Pallid Bat
p. 73

Townsend's Big-eared Bat
p. 73

Broad-footed Mole
p. 73

Trowbridge's Shrew
p. 74

Virginia Opossum
p. 74

BIRDS

Canada Goose
p. 77

Mallard
p. 77

Cinnamon Teal
p. 78

Northern Shoveler
p. 78

Lesser Scaup
p. 79

Surf Scoter
p. 79

Bufflehead
p. 80

Common Merganser
p. 80

Ruddy Duck
p. 81

Ring-necked Pheasant
p. 81

Wild Turkey
p. 82

Calfornia Quail
p. 82

9

BIRDS

Common Loon
p. 83

Pied-billed Grebe
p. 83

Eared Grebe
p. 83

Western Grebe
p. 84

Brown Pelican
p. 84

Double-crested Cormorant
p. 84

Great Blue Heron
p. 85

Great Egret
p. 85

Snowy Egret
p. 85

Turkey Vulture
p. 86

California Condor
p. 86

Osprey
p. 87

White-tailed Kite
p. 87

Bald Eagle
p. 87

Northern Harrier
p. 88

Sharp-shinned Hawk
p. 88

Cooper's Hawk
p. 88

Red-shouldered Hawk
p. 89

Red-tailed Hawk
p. 89

American Kestrel
p. 89

Peregrine Falcon
p. 90

Virgina Rail
p. 90

Common Moorhen
p. 90

American Coot
p. 91

Black-bellied
Plover, p. 91

Killdeer
p. 91

Black-necked Stilt
p. 92

American Avocet
p. 92

Spotted Sandpiper
p. 92

Greater Yellowlegs
p. 93

Ring-billed Gull
p. 93

California Gull
p. 93

Western Gull
p. 94

Caspian Tern
p. 94

Forster's Tern
p. 94

Marbled Murrelet
p. 95

Rock Pigeon
p. 95

Band-tailed Pigeon
p. 95

Mourning Dove
p. 96

Barn Owl
p. 96

Great Horned Owl
p. 96

Spotted Owl
p. 97

White-throated Swift
p. 97

Anna's Hummingbird
p. 97

Belted Kingfisher
p. 98

Acorn Woodpecker
p. 98

Red-breasted Sapsucker
p. 98

Nuttall's Woodpecker
p. 99

Downy Woodpecker
p. 99

Northern Flicker
p. 99

Pileated Woodpecker
p. 100

Western Wood-Pewee
p. 100

Black Phoebe
p. 100

Ash-throated Flycatcher
p. 101

Western Kingbird
p. 101

Loggerhead Shrike
p. 101

Hutton's Vireo
p. 102

Steller's Jay
p. 102

Western Scrub-Jay
p. 102

Black-billed Magpie
p. 103

American Crow
p. 103

Common Raven
p. 103

Horned Lark
p. 104

Cliff Swallow
p. 104

Barn Swallow
p. 104

Chestnut-backed Chickadee
p. 105

Oak Titmouse
p. 105

Bushtit
p. 105

White-breasted Nuthatch
p. 106

Bewick's Wren
p. 106

Ruby-crowned Kinglet
p. 106

Western Bluebird
p. 107

13

Hermit Thrush
p. 107

American Robin
p. 107

Wrentit
p. 108

European Starling
p. 108

Cedar Waxwing
p. 108

Orange-crowned Warbler
p. 109

Yellow-rumped Warbler
p. 109

Common Yellowthroat
p. 109

Western Tanager
p. 110

California Towhee
p. 110

Savannah Sparrow
p. 110

Fox Sparrow
p. 111

Song Sparrow
p. 111

White-crowned Sparrow
p. 111

Dark-eyed Junco
p. 112

Black-headed Grosbeak
p. 112

Red-winged Blackbird
p. 112

Western Meadowlark
p. 113

BIRDS

Brewer's Blackbird
p. 113

Brown-headed Cowbird
p. 113

House Finch
p. 114

Pine Siskin
p. 114

Lesser Goldfinch
p. 114

American Goldfinch
p. 115

House Sparrow
p. 115

AMPHIBIANS & REPTILES

California Newt
p. 117

California Tiger Salamander
p. 117

Long-tailed Salamander
p. 117

Great Basin Spadefoot
p. 118

Western Toad
p. 118

Coastal Tailed Frog
p. 118

Bullfrog
p. 119

Red-legged Frog
p. 119

Pacific Treefrog
p. 119

Western Pond Turtle
p. 120

Leatherback Sea Turtle
p. 120

Southern Alligator Lizard
p. 121

Sagebrush Lizard
p. 121

Western Fence Lizard
p. 121

Western Whiptail
p. 122

Western Skink
p. 122

Yellow-bellied Racer
p. 123

Western Rattlesnake
p. 123

Common Gartersnake
p. 123

Gophersnake
p. 124

Common Kingsnake
p. 124

California Whipsnake
p. 124

Rubber Boa
p. 125

Sharp-tailed Snake
p. 125

Chinook Salmon
p. 127

Cutthroat Trout
p. 127

Rainbow Trout
p. 127

Brook Trout
p. 128

Brown Trout
p. 128

Black Prickleback
p. 128

Blackeye Goby
p. 129

Blue Rockfish
p. 129

Lingcod
p. 129

Tidepool Sculpin
p. 130

Pacific Sanddab
p. 130

Giant Owl Limpet	Black Abalone	Black Tegula
p. 133	p. 133	p. 133

California Mussel	Lined Chiton	Sea Lemon
p. 134	p. 134	p. 134

Red Sea Cucumber	Bat Star	Ochre Sea Star
p. 135	p. 135	p. 135

Eccentric Sand Dollar	Purple Sea Urchin	Aggregating Anemone
p. 136	p. 136	p. 136

Giant Green Anemone	Orange Cup Coral	Purple Sponge
p. 137	p. 137	p. 137

Moon Jellyfish	Red Octopus	Giant Acorn Barnacle
p. 138	p. 138	p. 139

INVERTEBRATES

Barred Shrimp
p. 139

Dungeness Crab
p. 139

Purple Shore Crab
p. 140

Blue-handed Hermit Crab
p. 140

Western Tiger Swallowtail
p. 141

Monarch
p. 141

Spring Azure
p. 141

Orange Sulphur
p. 142

Clouded Sulphur
p. 142

California Dogface
p. 142

California Tortoiseshell
p. 142

California Silkmoth
p. 143

Snowberry Clearwing
p. 143

California Tent Caterpillar
Moth, p. 143

Boreal Bluet
p. 144

California Spreadwing
p. 144

Variegated Meadowhawk
p. 144

Pacific Tiger Beetle
p. 145

Golden Jewel Beetle
p. 145

Convergent Ladybug
p. 145

Yellow Jackets
p. 146

Bumble Bees
p. 146

Carpenter Ants
p. 146

Giant Crane Flies
p. 147

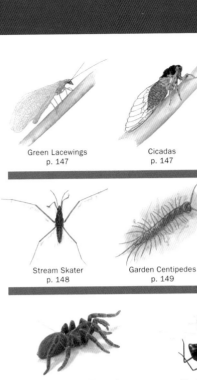

Green Lacewings
p. 147

Cicadas
p. 147

Angular-winged Katydid
p. 148

California Mantid
p. 148

Stream Skater
p. 148

Garden Centipedes
p. 149

Clown Millipede
p. 149

Garden Harvestmen
p. 149

California Ebony Tarantula
p. 150

Western Black Widow
p. 150

Yellow-orange Banana Slug
p. 150

White Fir
p. 153

Shore Pine
p. 153

Jeffrey Pine
p. 154

Sugar Pine
p. 154

Ponderosa Pine
p. 155

Douglas-fir
p. 155

Western Hemlock
p. 156

Incense Cedar
p. 156

Monterey Cypress
p. 157

Giant Sequoia
p. 157

Redwood
p. 158

Tanoak
p. 159

TREES

California Black Oak
p. 159

California Live Oak
p. 160

Red Alder
p. 160

Black Cottonwood
p. 161

Quaking Aspen
p. 161

Pacific Madrone
p. 162

Pacific Dogwood
p. 162

Oregon Ash
p. 163

California Boxelder
p. 163

SHRUBS

Juniper spp.
p. 166

Prince's-pine
p. 166

Falsebox
p. 166

Common Bearberry
p. 167

Salal
p. 167

Black Huckleberry
p. 167

False Azalea
p. 168

Pacific Rhododendron
p. 168

Whiteleaf Manzanita
p. 168

Scouler's Willow
p. 169

Red-osier Dogwood
p. 169

Western Mountain-ash
p. 169

Thimbleberry
p. 170

Ninebark
p. 170

Oceanspray
p. 170

Shrubby Cinquefoil
p. 171

Bitterbrush
p. 171

Chamise
p. 171

Scotch Broom
p. 172

Big Sagebrush
p. 172

Rabbitbush
p. 172

Deerbrush
p. 173

Cascara Buckthorn
p. 173

Bristly Black Currant
p. 173

Squaw Currant
p. 174

Common Snowberry
p. 174

Twinberry
p. 174

Black Elderberry
p. 175

Poison Oak
p. 175

California Buckeye
p. 175

Nodding Onion
p. 178

Mariposa Lily
p. 178

Corn Lily
p. 178

Chocolate Lily
p. 179

False Lily-of-the-valley
p. 179

Star-flowered False
Solomon's-seal, p. 179

Western Trillium
p. 180

California False-hellebore
p. 180

HERBS, FERNS & SEAWEEDS

Meadow Death Camas
p. 180

Skunk Cabbage
p. 181

Western Springbeauty
p. 181

Miner's Lettuce
p. 181

Threeleaf Lewisia
p. 182

Field Chickweed
p. 182

Seabluff Catchfly
p. 182

American Winter Cress
p. 183

Field Mustard
p. 183

Milk Maids
p. 183

Peppergrass
p. 184

California Poppy
p. 184

Pacific Bleeding Heart
p. 184

Small-flowered Woodland
Star, p. 185

Fringed Grass-of-Parnassus
p. 185

Brook Saxifrage
p. 185

Pacific Sedum
p. 186

Windflower
p. 186

Western Columbine
p. 186

Marsh Marigold
p. 187

Western Buttercup
p. 187

Meadowrue
p. 187

Beach Strawberry
p. 188

Redwood Sorrel
p. 188

Wood Violet
p. 188

Broad-leaf Lupine
p. 189

Clover
p. 189

Winter Vetch
p. 189

Fireweed
p. 190

Cow Parsnip
p. 190

Northern Gentian
p. 190

Western Waterleaf
p. 191

Baby Blue-eyes
p. 191

Varileaf Phacelia
p. 191

Spreading Phlox
p. 192

Toothed Downingia
p. 192

Pennyroyal
p. 192

Scarlet Paintbrush
p. 193

Yellow Monkeyflower
p. 193

David's Penstemon
p. 193

American Brooklime
p. 194

Common Yarrow
p. 194

Leafy Aster
p. 194

Brass Buttons
p. 195

Subalpine Fleabane
p. 195

Common Tarweed
p. 195

Woolly Mule Ears
p. 196

Heart-leaved Arnica
p. 196

HERBS, FERNS & SEAWEEDS

Sitka Valerian
p. 196

Bracken Fern
p. 197

Sword Fern
p. 197

Maidenhair Fern
p. 197

Surf Grass
p. 198

Turkish Towel
p. 198

Giant Kelp
p. 199

Bull Kelp
p. 199

Sea Lettuce
p. 199

Northern California contains a dramatic variety of landscapes, climates and biodiversity. Marine and coastal zones, rugged mountains, humid forests, wild backcountry, grasslands, sagebrush scrublands, deserts, streams and lakes all contribute to its unique, scenic wonders and ecological grandeur. Conservation International defines the California Floristic Province—the area of California west of the Sierra Nevada-Cascade Range—as a world biodiversity hotspot, owing to an unusual concentration of endemic plants. Of approximately 8000 plant species in the geographic region, about half are endemic. Many areas of Northern California, especially in the mountains, have been protected, and the significance of that foresight is inestimable.

Those of us lucky enough to live in or visit Northern California may be just minutes away from some of the most thrilling wildlife encounters in North America. In the bays and inlets along our coastline, we are able to see abundant marine life, and just offshore, passing whales frequently delight us. In protected remote areas, the presence of American black bears and mountain lions reminds us that parts of Northern California remain truly wild. Coyotes, deer, foxes, hawks, songbirds, bats, butterflies, frogs and snakes bring the "wild" right into our cities. Animals normally considered pests, such as pigeons, house sparrows and several insects, allow urban dwellers to appreciate the diversity of life in their otherwise lonely mono-species settings. Even bugs are wildlife, and there are over 20,000 species of insects here.

Northern California has several different bioregions and ecological provinces. Learning about these natural regions can help us understand the plants and animals living here and how they interact with us and with each other.

ECOLOGICAL PROVINCES AND BIOREGIONS

The Coast

Northern California's wonderfully irregular coastline has randomly distributed sandy or rocky beaches that are often closely backed by the steep foothills and headland ridges of the western slope of the Coast Range. This rugged scenery reaches its greatest expression in the Big Sur of southern Monterey County, and along the Lost Coast of northern Mendocino and southern Humboldt counties. Numerous small offshore islands, or "sea stacks," particularly north of San Francisco, provide nesting habitat for most of the region's breeding seabirds.

The Pacific Ocean

The Pacific Ocean offers habitat for pelagic seabirds and a diversity of marine life to thrill divers, sport fishers, birders and whale watchers. The deep water of the North Pacific Gyre beyond the continental slope remains fairly warm all year. Near-shore cold and warm currents, varying somewhat in temperature each year, bathe the continental shelf and influence prey availability for many species including coastal-breeding cormorants and western gulls. El Niño–Southern Oscillation events greatly influence the intensity of subtropical wintering migrants into our area.

The Klamath North Coast

This bioregion encompasses the rocky coastline and the Klamath and Siskiyou mountains. The Klamath Basin—not actually an enclosed basin, because the Klamath River flows out to the ocean—is on the route of the Pacific Flyway, a vitally strategic bird migratory route featuring waterfowl staging sites. The Klamath region receives the most rainfall of any part of the state.

Topography of Northern California

OREGON

Klamath
Mountains

CASCADE RANGE

Warner Mts

MODOC
PLATEAU

GREAT
BASIN

NEVADA

COAST RANGES

Sacramento Valley

Lake
Tahoe

Sacramento

SIERRA NEVADA

BASIN AND
RANGE

San
Francisco
Bay

Monterey
Bay

San Joaquin Valley

Inyo Mountains

Death Valley

CENTRAL COAST

Mojave
Desert

Los Angeles

Channel
Islands

San
Diego

Salton
Sea

Colorado River

Colorado Desert

ARIZONA

MEXICO

PACIFIC
OCEAN

Habitats of
Northern
California

- Mountains
- Deserts
- Grasslands / Agricultural
- Foothills
- Coastal Shrub / Chaparral
- Coastal Areas

The ecological province is defined by Coastal Steppe and mixed and redwood forests, and contains Redwood National Park, four national forests and several wilderness parks. A patchy belt of pine and cypress along the narrow coastal plain and sloping marine terraces lead to lush mixed coniferous forests at low elevations (below 3000 feet). The Klamath Mountains have the greatest concentration of conifer species on earth. White fir, Douglas-fir, ponderosa pine, shore pine, mountain hemlock, cedar and the famous redwoods and giant sequoia, with an understory of Pacific rhododendrons, azaleas, salal, huckleberry, sword fern and redwood sorrel, comprise the vegetation of this region. However, there are also distinct areas of dry, cold, shrubby uplands, a few broad valleys and grassland hills, coastal prairie shrub, coastal dune communities, aspen-lined lakes and rivers, and inland south-facing mountain slopes of tanoak, live oak and madrone mixed forest.

The wildlife in this region includes mule deer, Roosevelt elk (in Redwood National Forest), mountain lions, black bears, red and gray foxes, wolverines, northern river otters, northern flying squirrels, Douglas and western gray squirrels, chipmunks, Anna's hummingbirds, warblers, spotted owls, great-horned owls, marbled murrelets, salamanders, banana slugs and anadromous fish in the rivers and streams.

The Coast Range

The Coast Range is a series of mountain ranges with different origins and biogeography. These steeply sloping, low mountains—elevations range from 500 to 2500 feet (though some peaks rise to 5000 feet)—are underlain by shale, sandstone and igneous and volcanic rocks.

This ecological province is defined by open woodlands, shrublands, coniferous forest and meadows. Ridgelines and stream canyons angled northwest–southeast create sunny and shady areas, some seaward, others leeward. The northern portion of the Coast Range, like the Klamath, supports moist coniferous forests

dominated by coast redwood or Douglas-fir. Toward the south, mixed-species oak and conifer stands are interspersed with grassy hillsides and chaparral. The extreme southern reaches of the Coast Range become warmer and drier, supporting species characteristic of the northernmost habitats of southern California and the Mojave Desert. The eastern slopes of the Coast Range are drier and warmer in summer and support semi-arid oak-dotted grasslands leading to chaparral shrubs such as chamise and manzanita and evergreen oaks, then to pine and mixed-conifer forest.

The Coast Range provides habitat for mammals, including mule deer, coyote, mountain lion, bobcat, gray fox, woodrat, spotted and striped skunks, chipmunks and kangaroo rats. The diverse birdlife includes the wrentit, bushtit, white-crowned sparrow, fox sparrow, hermit thrush, ruby-crowned kinglet, warblers and the California condor. The coast horned lizard and gopher-snake and most of California's amphibians are encountered, but the Pacific treefrog is not.

Central Coast

Major landscape features in the Central Coast bio-region include coastal mountains, dunes and interior forests. Chaparral, mixed hardwood forests, redwood forests and oak woodlands support elk, mountain lion, long-tailed weasel, brush rabbit and western mastiff bat. Humpback and gray whales are seasonally common along the coast as they migrate either north to colder, food-rich waters, or south to warmer waters where they bear their calves. This bioregion supports a large human population and faces major problems owing to the effects of increasing urbanization and industry.

San Francisco Bay Area

The Bay Area of San Francisco is an ecological province defined by coastal chaparral forest and shrublands. Various habitats include low coastal mountains (elevation ranges from sea level to 2400 feet), interior valleys, salt marshes, redwood and mixed forests, coastal islands, freshwater marshes and coastal prairies.

Plant species found in this landscape include Monterrey cypress, live oak, redwoods, Douglas-fir and several species of pine, manzanita, sagebrush and lupines. Both salt and freshwater marshes are extremely important to migrating birds, and all the marsh zones are popular sites for birders and wildlife enthusiasts. The San Francisco Bay Area boasts a growing population of sea otters thanks to an excellent recovery program; other marine mammals include seals, sea-lions and whales. Terrestrial mammals that inhabit this region include the common gray fox, mule deer, bobcat, Virginia opossum and brush rabbit.

Central Valley

The San Joaquin Valley and the Sacramento Valley

The San Joaquin and Sacramento valleys comprise California's Central Valley, a flat alluvial plain between the Sierra Nevada to the east and Coast Range interior slopes to the west. Elevation ranges from sea level to 500 feet. The Sacramento Valley butts into the foothills of the southern Cascades; in the north is the watershed of the northern Sierra Nevada. The southern reaches of the San Joaquin Valley expire into the Mojave Desert. Sloping alluvial fans, slightly dissected terraces and the lower foothills of surrounding uplands border these broad valleys.

The two major waterways are the Sacramento and American rivers. They carry water to the Sacramento–San Joaquin River Delta, whose only natural outlet is to the San Francisco Bay system, which provides water for two-thirds of California's population. The Central Valley once supported fabulous riparian forests, but since its emergence as an agricultural center in the settlement era after the Gold Rush, its two master streams have been tamed and the riparia reduced to sorry remnants. The valley floor has been thoroughly altered, and the result is a patchwork of crop fields, orchards, fallow ground, towns, cities and other human developments.

Today, nearly none of the original grassland or marsh cover persists, and what remains is essential wintering habitat for many species of waterfowl, herons, egrets and birds of prey such as falcons and hawks. Within heavily managed sanctuaries, a thriving birdlife includes the mourning dove, horned lark, western meadowlark, western kingbird, loggerhead shrike, house finch, lesser goldfinch, red-shafted northern flicker, western scrub-jay, California quail, red-tailed hawk and Cooper's hawk. Among several species of reptiles, rattlesnakes are important predators of rodents. Mammals include the coyote, bobcat, mule deer, northern river otter, ringtail, common muskrat, badger, western pipistrelle, cottontails, black-tailed jackrabbits and kangaroo rats. The endemic San Joaquin kit fox is an endangered species in its namesake valley.

Cascade-Sierra Nevada Ranges

Cascade Range

The Cascade Range comprises a series of medium- to high-elevation ridges, with the rather uniform skyline broken here and there by eye-catching, spectacular peaks and deeply incised canyons. The range is situated beneath the Pacific storm track, and the western slopes are well watered. The region's original vigorous forests were perhaps more characteristic of the Pacific Northwest; they have been intensively "managed," yet regrowth is rapid in this area.

Plant diversity here is great, especially in the higher valleys and meadows of the southern fringe of the Cascades. The Klamath River is the only stream to completely bisect the range in California. The Cascades' eastern slopes are more arid, with Douglas-fir forest giving way to picturesque ponderosa pine, white fir and incense-cedar stands with an understory of bitterbrush, ceanothus, currant and manzanita. Lightning from summer thunderstorms has written a history in weathered charcoal on the trunks of innumerable ancient trees throughout the range. The parched and sprawling brushfields in the vicinity of Mt. Shasta feature an amazing array of colors and plant textures. Birds abound in the Cascades, especially in summer and particularly near wet meadow edges, where stands of trees contain numerous snags.

Sierra Nevada

The magnificent Sierra Nevada is a long and remarkably tall uplift that vividly separates two entirely distinct climates and contains the headwaters of rivers that generate much of California's water supply. Moist marine air masses arriving from the north Pacific rise, expand, cool and drop their moisture across the western slopes of the range. The clouds having been wrung dry, little precipitation falls east of the general summit of the Sierras. Much of this region has been glaciated, resulting in carved gorges of such grandeur and dimension that visitors from around the world flock to view them. The long west slope of the Sierra Nevada rises gradually from 2000 feet to over 14,000 feet. The east slope drops abruptly to the floor of the Great Basin, about 4000 feet. Mt. Whitney, at 14,496 feet, is the crown of the Sierra bioregion and the highest mountain in the contiguous United States. The numerous state parks and national forests include Yosemite National Park and the twin parks of Kings Canyon and Sequoia National Park.

Owing to its great range of elevation, its north-to-south extent and the meeting of "west-side" and "east-side" fauna and flora, the Sierra Nevada is biologically complex—it also contains more than half of the plant species known to occur in California. The mountain wildflowers in their full-blooming splendor are a spectacular sight to those lucky enough to see them. The oak and grassland habitats of the lower western slopes finger upward into scattered black oak and pine woodlands across a broken but broad front. The lower eastern slopes support plants and animals that are characteristic of the fringes of the Great Basin (in the north) and the northern Mojave Desert (in the south). The semi-arid plant communities of low hills are evergreen chaparral (mostly buckthorn and manzanita), which give way to typical Sierran conifer forests of white fir, sugar pine, Douglas-fir, ponderosa pine, Jeffrey pine, incense cedar and giant sequoia. In turn, semi-open and clumped stands of subalpine trees, such as mountain hemlock and lodgepole pine, reach their limit around the edges of the abundant glacial basins and snow-fed tarns below the crest of the range. The arid and winter-chilled higher elevations of the eastern front are characterized by juniper woodlands, and white fir and aspen stands. The highest ridgelines and peaks of the range stand boulder-strewn, windswept and nearly barren.

Like the plant diversity, the animal diversity in this bioregion is also very high; up to two-thirds of California's mammals can be found here. The bighorn sheep, mule deer, American black bear, coyote, red fox, fisher, porcupine, wolverine, fisher and mountain lion are some of the most charismatic species here, and abundant smaller mammals include the mountain beaver, golden-mantled ground squirrel, bushytail woodrat, flying squirrel and Trowbridge's shrew. Birdlife includes Hammond's flycatcher, Audubon's warbler, pine siskin, Cooper's hawk and the great gray owl.

Modoc Plateau/Great Basin

Modoc Bioregion

Pioneers on their way to California first crossed the Great Basin and Modoc Plateau more than 150 years ago. Few stayed, and the Modoc bioregion still has the lowest human population in all of California. Much of the rugged landscape of the Modoc Plateau was born of extensive lava flows from volcanic activity in prehistory, and cinder cones and lava caves can still be seen. The most recent volcanic activity in Lassen Volcanic National Park, which contains the towering 10,457-foot Lassen Peak, occurred in 1915. Elsewhere in this bioregion are the Modoc and Lassen national forests and part of the Klamath National Forest.

This region is mostly semi-arid, with stands of trees restricted chiefly to the foothills and mountain slopes. The dominant forest vegetation includes ponderosa pine, Jeffery pine, white fir, cedars and aspen. The "basin-and-range" topography so associated with the Great Basin is easily perceived here; a sea of tall and low sagebrush, as well as rabbitbrush, remnant native bunchgrasses, native and exotic annual grasses and many colorful wildflowers and forbs, is banked by a western fringe of juniper and pinyon pine woodlands.

Animals in this region include the pronghorn, mule deer, bighorn sheep and even the elusive mink. Birdlife is varied and abundant in both the mountain forest habitat of the isolated Warner Mountains and the alkaline basins and saline lakes. Surface water is rare, but nesting colonies and migratory staging grounds for waterfowl and waders are found where wetlands and lakes occur; Mono Lake, Honey Lake and Goose Lake are the most significant lakes in this region.

HUMAN IMPACT ON NORTHERN CALIFORNIA'S LANDSCAPE

The impact of humans on natural environments is visible throughout Northern California, and no outline of its important habitats would be complete without mention its towns, cities, roads, agricultural areas and forestry and mining sites. The pattern of settlement in Northern California is irregular, with the population most densely clustered around the San Francisco Bay Area and smaller cities scattered throughout the Central Valley. Agricultural development is high in the wine-producing counties of Napa and Sonoma, and in the fertile San Joaquin Valley, the leading fruit- and vegetable-producing region in the state. Along the coast and much more sparingly east of the mountains are still more towns.

Biodiversity is highest along the suburban fringe, where a botanical anarchy of remnant native plants, exotic introduced plants and hybrids exist. Strategic species, whether native or introduced, take advantage of evolving opportunities for food, shelter and breeding territory. We have built bird feeders, birdhouses, bat houses, lakes and urban parks to accommodate the species we appreciate, while wharves and ports, garbage dumps and our homes attract the species we consider pests. Many of the most common plants and animals in these altered landscapes are non-native species that came on the heels of settlement and with modern transportation needs. In fact, California is one of the states with the highest number of introduced species.

THE SEASONS

California's climate and seasons influence plants and animals. Aside from airborne creatures such as bats and birds, or marine species such as whales and fish, most species are confined to relatively slow forms of getting around. As a result, they have limited geographic ranges and must cope with the changing seasons. Water has the most critical influence on vegetation, determining availability of food and shelter. Average annual precipitation is directly affected by landform, with coastal or windward slopes receiving the greatest share of it. 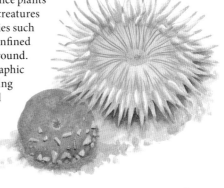 As we have seen, landforms in northern California are complex and diverse, thus rainfall and snowfall may vary dramatically in only a few miles.

California is known for its warm climate, especially in winter. In the south and along the coast, winter is not terribly stressful on plant or animal life. However, in northern and alpine areas, winter is a sparse and cold season with significant snowfall. Some animals must eat vast quantities of food in the summer to build up fat reserves, and others work furiously to stockpile food caches in safe places. The life cycles of yet other species end come winter, leaving spring for the next generation. Summers may be a time of growth and recovery from winter, or a time of stress from heat and aridity.

An important aspect of seasonality is its effect on species composition. Some migratory species head south for warmer climes at the same time as other migratory species from the Arctic are entering our area for the winter. When you visit the Northern California mountain regions in winter, you will observe different species than in summer. Many species, such as ground squirrels and American black bears, are dormant in winter. Many ungulates may be more visible in winter because they enter lowland meadows to find edible vegetation. For some of the more charismatic species, fall is the time for mating. At this time of year, male bighorn sheep are more noticeable as they demonstrate extremes of aggression and vigilance.

The north and central coast climate—mild with cool summers and winters never below freezing—is influenced by seasonal rains. There is zero rainfall in this gentle climate in midsummer, but annual rainfall totals 40 to 100 inches. Heavy fogs are common on the coast; the north coast region has a greater mean number of days with dense fogs than any other place in the United States. The Bay Area's year-round climate is humid. Summers tend to be warm or cool and sometimes foggy, and winters are usually cool but mild and rainy. On very rare occasions, there may be wet, short-lived snowfalls.

35

The Coast Range has hot, dry summers and rainy, mild winters; moisture in summer comes mainly from fog. Lightning commonly sets fires in chaparral and shrub areas. The eastern interior part of the Klamath bioregion has less rain and hotter, drier summers than the coastal zones. Summers fluctuate between heat waves at over 100°F, and cooling delta breezes that come in from the Bay Area.

The seasons in the Central Valley are more pronounced than on the coast, but they are milder than in the Sierras. Summers are hot and winters mild, often foggy, with some rain but little or no snow. The upper San Joaquin Valley receives precipitation only during winter storms and occasional summer showers; annual rainfall is approximately 6 inches compared to the coast, which receives nearly 30 inches. Winters tend to be moist with heavy fog, while summers are long, hot and dry. Sacramento Valley winters are cool, but snow rarely falls because the temperatures are usually above freezing; winter white comes in the form of heavy fog, from about Thanksgiving through until the end of February.

Elevation differences throughout the Sierra Nevada make for climates that differ greatly from one place to the next. At high elevations, winters tend to be snowy and cold, while winters at low elevations are rainy and cool. Summers everywhere tend to be quite dry, but high elevations are still only cool to warm. The base of the western slope gets 10 to 15 inches of rain per year with a long, dry summer, while higher elevations have a shorter summer and higher precipitation (to 70 inches), often as snow. Moisture carried on west winds from the coast cannot pass the high ranges, leaving the eastern slopes much drier, with most precipitation in winter in the form of snow at higher elevations.

Winter in the isolated Modoc region means snow in high-elevation areas and cool rains and frost in low-elevation areas, and summers throughout the bioregion are hot and dry.

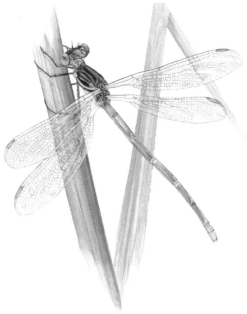

OBSERVING NATURE

Viewing Wildlife

Many species of wildlife are most easily encountered at dawn and dusk, when they come out from their daytime hideouts or roosting sites, so the best times for viewing are during these "wildlife hours." During winter, hunger may force certain mammals to be more active during midday. Conversely, in warm seasons, some animals may become less active and less visible in the heat of the day. Within the protected reserves and national parks of Northern California, many larger mammals can be viewed easily from the safety of a vehicle. On backcountry trails, however, you are in their territory, and close encounters are best avoided.

Whale Watching

Whale watching can either be an organized activity, with boats taking groups of tourists out to known areas of high whale and dolphin sightings, or it can be a random moment of fortune right from the shore. Remember that although whale watching can increase public awareness and appreciation for marine mammals and the health of the oceans, it can disrupt cetacean behavior. Tour groups must be considerate and passive in the presence of these sensitive species.

Birding

Birding is an increasingly popular activity that allows us to appreciate diversity and beauty in nature. It offers people potential moments of inspiration and sheer refreshment throughout their lives. There are scores of excellent guidebooks, and a burgeoning body of literature and portraiture available online and through clubs and organizations. Practiced with patience and reserve, birding is a minimally consumptive devotion that respects, rather than degrades, the environment. Watching birds is a ready source of mental and physical exercise; with perhaps 450 species either resident or migrating through, Northern California offers endless exploration and satisfaction for serious birders and novices alike. One must be patient, though, because birds are among the most highly mobile animals on the planet; seen clearly and closely one moment, they can be gone the next!

Humans and Wildlife

Although people have generally become more conscious of the need to protect wildlife, the pressures of increased human visitation have nevertheless damaged critical habitats. Modern wildlife viewing demands courtesy, respect and common sense. Here are some points to remember for ethical wildlife watching:

- Stress is harmful to wildlife, so never chase or flush animals from cover or try to catch or touch them. Use binoculars and keep your distance, for the animal's sake and for your own.

- Leave the environment unchanged by your visit. Tread lightly, and take home only pictures and memories. Do not pick wildflowers, and do not collect sea stars, sea urchins or seashells still occupied by the animal. Amphibians are especially sensitive to being touched or held, and sunscreen and insect repellant on your skin can poison the animal.

- Pets might chase, injure or kill wildlife, so control your pets or leave them at home.

- Take the time to learn about wildlife and the behavior and sensitivity of each species.

NATIONAL PARKS IN NORTHERN CALIFORNIA

Yosemite National Park

Perhaps California's most famous national park, Yosemite is an excellent destination for visitors interested in dramatic scenery and unbeatable wildlife encounters. Located in the central Sierra Nevada, this park contains thousands of lakes and ponds, rugged mountains, 1600 miles of streams and 800 miles of hiking trails. Famous landmark features include El Capitan, the world's largest granite monolith, the 620-foot high Bridal Veil Falls and the impressive Half Dome. At 8842 feet in height, this 87-million-year-old piece of plutonic rock dominates most of Yosemite Valley's views. Hetch Hetchy Valley was flooded by the construction of the infamous O'Shaughnessy Dam, the protest against which was one of the greatest conservation battles in history, and John Muir's last before his death a year after the battle was lost. He had described this valley as "a grand landscape garden, one of Nature's rarest and most precious mountain temples." The area surrounding the reservoir is still popular for hiking and is fascinating from both an engineering and historical perspective—controversy dominates the debate on whether to remove the dam and return the valley to its natural state. The park's bioregions include chaparral-oak woodlands and lower and upper montane, subalpine and alpine zones. As well, you may find yourself venturing into rare and magnificent sequoia groves amid the forests of California black oak, ponderosa pine and incense cedar. Mariposa lilies and woolly mule ears are two of the many flowers to look for. Yosemite is an area of habitat for over 300 wildlife species, including mountain lions, black bears, bighorn sheep, coyotes, western gray squirrels and several breeding pairs of peregrine falcons.

Lassen Volcanic National Park

Lassen Peak is the largest of a group of some 30 volcanic domes in the Cascade Range, which have been active over the past 300,000 years. Steam and volcanic gasses are blown to the surface by the fiery giant that slumbers here deep inside the earth. The steam- and gas-spewing vents are known as fumaroles, and along with mud pots and geysers, they make this park a dramatic and energetic place to visit. The last eruption exploded violently on May 22, 1915, at Lassen Peak, the southernmost active volcano in the Cascades. Volcanic ash was spewed as far as 200 miles to the east. Part of the same tectonic system, Lava Beds National Monument lies on the northeast flank of Medicine Lake Volcano, the largest volcano in the Cascade Range. It is an active shield volcano that has erupted numerous times over the past half-million years, forming a stark landscape of black, dried lava, smooth and rippling in some areas, jagged and aggressive in others. From this seemingly uninhabitable setting, however, spring up colorful wildflowers, including the California poppy, contrasting against their black backdrop, and western fence lizards and western rattlesnakes relish sunning themselves on the sun-heated rocks. The most interesting features are the hundreds of lava tube caves to explore—the largest concentration of lava tubes in North America. Many species of lichens, mosses and ferns, such as the sword fern, grow in the moist caves, oddly enough finding themselves in a desert climate far from their typically coastal habitats. Of course, the most expected cave dweller, the bat, is represented by several species, some of which form large colonies in these caves. Care must be taken so as not to disturb roosting colonies, especially in winter. Surrounding the rocky strata are sagebrush grasslands, juniper-pine brushlands and pine forests, each of which hosts a unique array of wildlife species.

Death Valley National Park

Despite its foreboding name, Death Valley can be an exciting place for a holiday. The national park covers over 3 million acres of western desert, and elevations range from the Badwater Basin saltpan at 282 feet below sea level to the summit of Telescope Peak at 11,049 feet. This park includes many extreme zones such as saltpans, subalpine and even some regions that rank among the hottest and driest places on earth. All of the species of animals and plants found here exhibit adaptations to help them survive in extreme conditions.

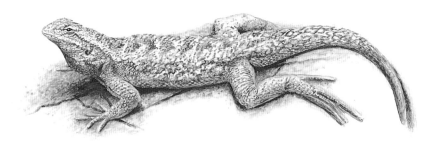

National Parks in Northern California

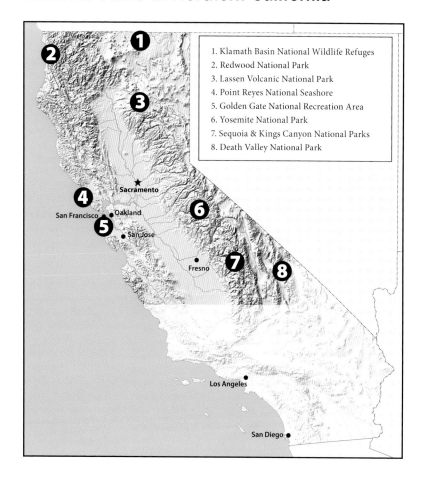

1. Klamath Basin National Wildlife Refuges
2. Redwood National Park
3. Lassen Volcanic National Park
4. Point Reyes National Seashore
5. Golden Gate National Recreation Area
6. Yosemite National Park
7. Sequoia & Kings Canyon National Parks
8. Death Valley National Park

Point Reyes National Seashore

The spectacularly beautiful Point Reyes National Seashore encompasses rugged coastline, open beaches and rolling mountains that resemble a Mediterranean ecosystem. The Point Reyes Lighthouse was completed in 1870, and for over 135 years, it has endured the elements and guided ships along what is considered the foggiest part of the coast. Forests within the park include bishop pine and Douglas-fir communities. Numerous species of dolphins and whales can be seen from the mainland. Point Reyes is an excellent place for viewing and photographing northern elephant seals, which have made a comeback here since 1970. Prior to 1970, hunting had decimated their populations. Occasionally, large groups of juvenile loggerhead sea turtles have been observed feeding on blooms of jellyfish close to shore. At the start of winter, when the rainy season begins, Coho and steelhead salmon begin to converge at the mouths of creeks and rivers to make their impressive journeys upstream to spawn—care must be taken not to disturb them at this extremely sensitive and important period of their life cycle. A local nonprofit organization called SPAWN (Salmon Protection and Watershed Network) works to protect these endangered species but offers walks to view them during the spawning season. There are over 1000 species of plants and animals in this protected area for visitors to potentially see.

Klamath Basin National Wildlife Refuges

This union of six wildlife refuges encompasses extensive wetland, meadow and forest habitats. Three of the refuges are located in Oregon, while Lower Klamath, Tule Lake and Clear Lake refuges lie mostly in California. The mixed habitat is home to a wide diversity of birds, amphibians and mammals. Seventy-eight species of mammals are known or suspected to occur in or near the Klamath refuges, among which are several species of bats of the *Myotis* genus, red and gray foxes, coyotes, raccoons, skunks, beavers, mule deer and pronghorns. Eared and western grebes are common in summer, Canada geese and northern shovelers come here to breed, and the American coot and red-winged blackbird are almost guaranteed sightings at any time of year. Long-toed salamanders, western toads, pacific treefrogs and bullfrogs make a chorus of amphibian life alongside reptiles such as the western pond turtle.

Sequoia and Kings Canyon National Parks

Sequoia was California's first official national park. It was formed in 1890, exactly 50 years before its counterpart, Kings Canyon, was established. The two adjoining parks are managed as one. The parks boast an enormous elevation range, from 1360 feet to 14,491 feet, which encompasses a wide diversity of ecosystems and wildlife. The dominant plant communities include groves of giant sequoia, vast tracts of montane forests, spectacular alpine habitats and chaparral-oak woodlands. The forest is often raucous with the cawing of ravens and squawking of Steller's jays; interspersed among their bantering is the more delicate twittering and singing of the mountain chickadee. Many of the mammals change their habits in winter here; black bears can be seen at high elevations in winter, at which time the mule deer move into the valleys in greater densities to forage and avoid heavy snow, in which you may see jackrabbit or bobcat tracks. In spring, the foothills are covered in wildflowers, the most obvious blankets of color typically offered by the lupines, and in the heat of summer, western rattlesnakes can sometimes be seen sunning themselves on exposed rocks.

Redwood National and State Parks

The Redwood parks comprise several parks united into one protected area. The parks include Prairie Creek Redwoods State Park, Del Norte Coast Redwoods State Park, Jebediah Smith Redwoods State Park and Redwood National Park. Together these parks are a World Heritage Site and an International Biosphere Reserve. The Redwood parks protect 45 percent of all the old-growth redwood forest remaining in California. Redwood trees can live to be 2000 years old and stand over 300 feet tall. Protecting these trees has other conservation benefits. This park contains over 104,000 acres of land, including prairie and oak woodlands. The Redwood parks also protect the coast and seaside submerged area, totaling nearly 6000 acres. Within the park you may encounter Roosevelt elk, black bears and banana slugs or, with a stroke of luck, the rare marbled murrelet, which survives within these protected old-growth forests of redwoods and Douglas-fir. On the shore, you can find sea anemones in the tide pools or, on the watery horizon, see the blow of a gray whale as it passes. In the streams and rivers that flow to this coast, you may witness the runs of Chinook salmon as they head upstream to their spawning grounds.

Golden Gate National Recreation Area

One of the largest urban national parks in the world, the Golden Gate NRA was established in 1972. Covering 75,398 acres, the park extends from Tomales Bay in Marin County south to San Mateo County, and also includes 59 miles of shoreline, making it one of the nation's largest coastal preserves. Here you can watch sea otters playing in the tall kelp forests or eating sea urchins, while gulls and terns fly overhead and sandpipers probe the wet sand in search of small crustaceans. Within the park is Muir Woods National Monument. On January 9, 1908, President Theodore Roosevelt set aside Muir Woods to protect the groves of giant trees in the nearly 300 acres of the Tamalpais Sequoias. The land was donated by a private landowner in Redwood Canyon, William Kent, to the federal government for all future generations of Americans to enjoy. Roosevelt offered to name the park Kent Woods, an honor that Mr. Kent humbly declined, stating that this would suggest the purchasability of something that should belong to all. Today, you can still visit these groves and see the old giant sequoias and the animal species that live within the groves. The shady conditions created by these great trees limit the diversity of plant species and thus food for many animals, but several species of birds such as owls and mammals such as bats (11 species) do well in this dense, protective environment from which they can fly beyond to hunt. The spotted owl relies on old-growth to survive, which is what involved this unassuming species in the owls-vs.-jobs debate over protecting old-growth forests along the West Coast. Mule deer also seek refuge near the forest edges. The pileated woodpecker is another icon of the old-growth forest, and reptiles such as the western gartersnake and the rubber boa and shade-loving amphibians such as salamanders and newts also make their homes here. In naming Muir Woods National Monument, William Kent chose to honor John Muir, who dedicated his life to the protection of nature; he is called the "Father of the National Park Service," was the founder of the Sierra Club and inspired people through his writings, teachings and advocacy. The Victorian home of this famed conservationist is located in Martinez, California, and has been established as the John Muir National Historic Site. The original 2600-acre ranch has been sectioned and sold, but the home remains surrounded by almost 9 acres of fruit orchards and 326 acres of oak woodland.

ANIMALS

A nimals are mammals, birds, reptiles, amphibians, fish and invertebrates, all of which belong to the Kingdom Animalia. They obtain energy by ingesting food that they hunt or gather. Mammals and birds are endothermic, meaning that body temperature is internally regulated and will stay nearly constant despite the surrounding environmental temperature unless that temperature is extreme and persistent. Reptiles, amphibians, fish and invertebrates are ecto-thermic, meaning that they do not have the ability to generate their own internal body temperature and tend to be the same temperature as their surroundings. Animals reproduce sexually, and they have a limited growth that is reached at sexual maturity. They also have diverse and complicated behaviours displayed in courtship, defense, parenting, playing, fighting, eating, hunting, in their social hierarchy, and in how they deal with environmental stresses such as weather, change of season or availability of food and water.

MAMMALS

Mammals are the group to which human beings belong. The general characteristics of a mammal include being endothermic, bearing live young (with the exception of echidnas and the platypus), nursing their young and having hair or fur on their bodies. In general, all mammals larger than rodents are sexually dimorphic, meaning that the male and the female are different in appearance by size or other diagnostics such as antlers. Males are usually larger than females. Different groups of mammals are either herbivores, carnivores, omnivores or insectivores. People often associate large mammals with wilderness, making these animals prominent symbols in native legends and stirring emotional connections with people in modern times.

Hoofed Mammals
pp. 48–50

Cats
p. 51

Bears
p. 52

Dogs
pp. 52–53

Whales & Dolphins
pp. 54–57

Seals & Sea-Lions
pp. 58–59

Otters & Kin
p. 60

Weasels & Skunks
pp. 61–63

Raccoons
p. 63

Porcupine
p. 64

Beavers
p. 64

Mice & Kin
pp. 65–66

Squirrels
pp. 67–68

Hares & Rabbits
pp. 68–70

Pika
p. 70

Bats
pp. 70–73

Moles & Shrews
pp. 73–74

Opossum
p. 74

Bighorn Sheep

Ovis canadensis

Length: 5–6 ft (tail 3–5 in)
Shoulder height: 30–45 in
Weight: 120–340 lb

Icons of North American wilderness, male bighorn sheep are well known for their spectacular head-butting clashes during fall rut. Both sexes have brown horns, but males' are thick and curved forward. • Bighorn sheep are native to mountainous regions of Northern California; mountain meadows provide bighorns with feeding grounds, and rocky outcroppings provide protection from predators, namely eagles, mountain lions and bobcats, which prey on the lambs. **Where found:** rugged mountain slopes, cliffs and alpine meadows; some populations in rolling foothills; range extends from California north to the Rocky Mountains of Canada. **Also known as:** mountain sheep.

Pronghorn

Antilocapra americana

Length: 4–5 ft (tail 3½–6 in)
Shoulder height: 32–41 in
Weight: 70–140 lb

Often incorrectly referred to as an antelope, the pronghorn is actually the sole member of the family Antilocapridae (true antelopes belong to the Bovidae family along with cows, goats and sheep). Its branched horns are shed like antlers. • The pronghorn is the fastest animal in the Western Hemisphere, able to retain continuous 20-ft bounds at up to 60 mph, yet it cannot jump a fence. Fences in managed pronghorn territory are higher so the animals can duck underneath, which they can do at a full run without breaking stride. **Where found:** the grasslands of the Modoc Plateau.

Elk

Cervus elaphus

Length: 6–9 ft (tail 4½–7 in)
Shoulder height: 4–5 ft
Weight: 400–1000 lb

The haunting, high-pitched bugle calls of rutting male elk are a hallmark of fall in Northern California. A male's large, spreading antlers may span 5 ft and weigh up to 30 lb. During fall rut and in spring when females are with calves, elk can be very dangerous and should be avoided. • Elk tend to be shy forest dwellers, moving to open meadows at dusk to feed until dawn. • There are 3 subspecies of elk in Northern California: Rocky Mountain (*C. e. nelsoni*), Roosevelt (*C. e. roosevelti*) and tule (*C. e. nannodes*). Each one has slight variances in color and size. **Where found:** mixed forests, coniferous forests, mountain meadows and lake shorelines up to the timberline; throughout the Rockies. Roosevelt elk are coastal in range; Rocky Mountain elk are found mainly in Shasta County; tule elk are found in scattered populations in the south-central counties. **Also known as:** wapiti.

Mule Deer

Odocoileus hemionus

Length: 4–6 ft (tail 4½–9 in)
Shoulder height: 3–3½ ft
Weight: 68–470 lb

Mule deer form large bands, particularly in winter. They prefer hilly terrain, where they use bounding hops, like those of jackrabbits, called "stotting" or "pronking" to escape predators. • These deer are named for their very large, mule-like ears. Large ears and a black-tipped tail are the best field marks for this ungulate. • There are 6 subspecies of mule deer in Northern California, with various ranges.
Where found: from dry brushlands to high tundra; riparian areas in dry regions; young forests; throughout California. Bucks tend to remain at higher elevations while does and fawns stay at lower elevations. **Also known as:** black-tailed deer.

Feral Horse

Equus caballus

Length: up to 7 ft (tail up to 3 ft)
Shoulder height: 3½–5½ ft
Weight: 590–860 lb

Although the domesticated horse is common across North America, wild horses spark the romantic imagination of many people who see this introduced species as a symbol of freedom and a vestige of what remains wild in the West. Feral horses are descendants of domestic horses but have run wild for hundreds of years, from the Rocky Mountains to the Southwest. • Wild horses are distinguishable from domestic horses by their long manes and tails and by their pronounced behavioral patterns between members of the herd. **Where found:** small populations occur east of the Sierra Nevadas. **Also known as:** mustang.

Feral Pig

Sus scrofa

Length: 4½–6 ft
(tail up to 12 in)
Shoulder height: 21–43 in
Weight: *Male:* 165–440 lb;
Female: 77–330 lb

One typically thinks of a chubby, pink, bald, docile animal when envisioning a pig. Pigs were bred to lose many of their wild features, which include a coarse, dense fur coat, long, straight, sparsely furred tails and tusks (or modified canines). However, that domestic pig is the same species as its wild relative that was introduced to North America from Europe and Asia. The wild pig is not docile in its demeanor, either, but dangerously aggressive. • Wild and domestic pigs have hybridized in California, although "purebred" feral pigs still range. **Where found:** forested mountain areas in parks and preserves. **Also known as:** wild boar, wild pig, wild hog.

Mountain Lion

Felis concolor

Length: 5–9 ft (tail 25–32 in)
Shoulder height: 26–32 in
Weight: 70–190 lb

The powerful, majestic mountain lion is a large, secretive cat. The mountain lion is seldom seen by people, but studies over the past 30 years estimate the population by studying densities within different habitat types around the state, which vary from zero to 10 lions per 100 mi². Expanding the densities over the total amount of each habitat type available provides a crude estimate of 4000–6000 mountain lions statewide. • More than half of California is prime habitat for this cat—it is found wherever mule deer are present. Mountain lions often hunt by sitting in trees above animal trails waiting to pounce on prey. **Where found:** foothills and mountains from low-elevation valleys to treeline. **Also known as:** cougar, puma.

Bobcat

Lynx rufus

Length: 2½–4 ft (tail 5–7 in)
Shoulder height: 17–20 in
Weight: 15–29 lb

The nocturnal bobcat feeds on a wide range of prey, including rabbits, voles, mice, birds, reptiles and insects. Small but mighty, the bobcat is even capable of bringing down a deer by the throat if the opportunity presents itself. • This cat's atypically short "bobbed" tail is well suited to the shrubby and forested areas in which it hunts, but the bobcat is highly adaptable and may even be seen close to residential areas. • Like most young cats, bobcat kittens are almost always at play. **Where found:** coniferous and deciduous forests, brushy areas and riparian areas; all parts of chaparral country.

American Black Bear

Ursus americanus

Length: 4½–6 ft (tail 3–7 in)
Shoulder height: 3–4 ft
Weight: 88–595 lb

The black bear's pelage is most commonly black but varies to cinnamon brown and to honey blond, with a lighter-colored muzzle. This omnivore eats plant material and obtains protein from insects such as bees (often while on honey raids), scavenged meat or, rarely, hunting small mammals. The black bear spends winter in a den, but the hibernation is not deep, and the bear may rouse from its torpor and exit the den on mild winter days. • Although emblematic and on the state flag, the grizzly bear (*U. arctos horribilis*) is extirpated from California; the last one was shot in 1922 but became the state mammal nonetheless in 1953. **Where found:** throughout most forested regions of Northern California.

Coyote

Canis latrans

Length: 3½–4½ ft (tail 12–16 in)
Shoulder height: 23–26 in
Weight: 18–44 lb

Coyotes occasionally form loose packs and join in spirited yipping choruses. These intelligent and versatile hunter-scavengers are best described as opportunistic omnivores. They have been observed fishing or even engaging the help of a hunting badger to catch ground squirrels. • Once extirpated from California, along with the wolf, the coyote has made a comeback, and because of its adaptable and cunning behavior, it has thrived. **Where found:** mixed and coniferous forests, meadows, agricultural lands and suburban areas; almost every valley and most cities host a population of coyotes.

Gray Fox

Urocyon cinereoargenteus

Length: 30–43 in (tail 11–17 in)
Shoulder height: 14–15 in
Weight: 7½–13 lb

Preferring rocky, shrub-covered and forested terrain and avoiding populated areas, the mainly nocturnal gray fox is the most common fox in California, yet it is seldom seen unless you know where to look for it. • Most remarkable is this fox's ability to climb trees—the only member of the dog family able to do so—to escape danger, pursue birds or find egg-filled nests. It may even use a high tree-hollow for a den. • The gray fox's fur is shorter and denser than that of the red fox. **Where found:** open forests, shrublands and rocky areas.

Kit Fox

Vulpes macrotis

Length: 24–33 in (tail 9–13 in)
Shoulder height: 12 in
Weight: 3–6 lb

This housecat-sized fox does a great service to farmers and rural residents in keeping insect, such as grasshopper and locust, and rodent populations in check. This great mouser's service has not been acknowledged in return. The kit fox is erroneously perceived as vermin and has been extirpated from much of its former range, even today still falling victim to poaching and poisoning by land owners intolerant of wildlife. • The San Joaquin kit fox (*V. m. mutica*) is an endangered species, threatened by habitat loss from agricultural and urban development in the valley that is its namesake. **Where found:** sagebrush and grassland habitats in the San Joaquin Valley.

Red Fox

Vulpes vulpes

Length: 3–3½ ft (tail 14–17 in)
Shoulder height: 15 in
Weight: 8–15 lb

The red fox is a talented mouser with high-pouncing antics that are much more cat-like than dog-like. The entertaining, extroverted behavior and noble good looks of the red fox have landed it roles in many fairy tales, fables and native legends. • The red fox is typically a vivid reddish orange, but its coat has darker color phases with dark fur across the back and shoulders, or it can be almost entirely black with silver-tipped hairs. The tip of its elegant, bushy tail, however, is always white. **Where found:** open, grassy habitats with brushy shelter, riparian areas and forest edges; avoids dense forests.

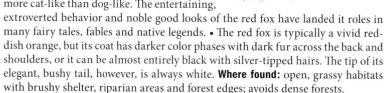

Gray Whale

Eschrichtius robustus

Length: average 45 ft; up to 50 ft
Weight: average 35 tons; up to 45 tons

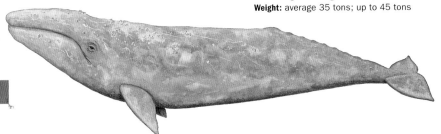

The sole member of the gray whale family, this baleen whale lacks the significant throat pleating of the rorqual whales. Its gray skin is covered with a speckling of barnacles and carries large communities of other organisms, such as whale lice, along for the ride. • The gray whale is famous for its lengthy migrations that take it between the arctic seas in summer and the Mexican coast in winter, thrilling whale watchers along the entire Pacific Coast as they pass by. **Where found:** generally coastal waters, as it migrates close to shore. **Also known as:** devilfish, mussel-digger, scrag whale.

Minke Whale

Balaenoptera acutorostrata

Length: average 27 ft; up to 35 ft
Weight: average 10 tons; up to 15 tons

Smallest of the rorquals—baleen whales with throats of pleated, expandable skin—the minke whale is occasionally seen in our waters, but it spends little time at the water surface, so a fleeting glimpse is a lucky one. • The minke whale has been one of the more heavily hunted of the baleen whales since the 1980s, when larger whale populations had already collapsed. **Where found:** open water, sometimes in bays, inlets and estuaries; migrates seasonally between warm and cold waters. **Also known as:** piked whale, sharp-headed finner, little finner, lesser fin-back, lesser rorqual.

Fin Whale

Balaenoptera physalus

Length: average 70 ft; up to 89 ft
Weight: average 80 tons;
up to 140 tons

When this long, sleek giant swims leisurely and gracefully along the surface of the water, its tall, narrow, dense blow reaches up to 20 ft high and is very noticeable on the horizon, but it does not show its fluke when beginning a dive. • The fin whale is found singly or in pairs, but more often in pods of 3–7 individuals. On occasion, several pods have been observed in a small area, creating concentrations of as many as 50 animals. • Fin whales are exceptionally fast movers and have been clocked at 20 mph in short bursts. **Where found:** offshore.

Humpback Whale

Megaptera novaeangliae

Length: average 45 ft; up to 62 ft
Weight: average 30 tons; up to 53 tons

The haunting songs of humpbacks can last from a few minutes to a few hours or even be epic, days-long concerts; they have inspired both scientists and artists and reach out to the imaginations of many people who listen and wonder what these great creatures are saying. • These rorquals employ a unique hunting strategy. They make a bubble net to round their prey into a tight cluster, thereby obtaining a food-dense gulp. **Where found:** off our shores in summer; migrates in winter to the waters off Mexico or Costa Rica, or to Hawaii to mate and calve.

Orca

Orcinus orca

Length: average 28 ft; up to 32 ft
Weight: average 7½ tons; up to 11 tons

Few people would not recognize this iconic creature that is found around the world. It is revered in legend and as a totem by Native Americans, celebrated by enthusiastic whale watchers and, unfortunately, cheered on for entertainment in captivity. • Researchers have identified 3 distinct types of killer whale along the Pacific Coast: transients, residents and offshore types. Transients and residents differ in many ways, including home range size, morphology, hunting preferences and social behavior; offshore types are similar to residents but range farther from the coast. Residents are less commonly observed in our area. **Where found:** cooler coastal waters, inshore and offshore. **Also known as:** killer whale.

Bottlenose Dolphin

Tursiops truncatus

Length: average 10 ft; up to 13 ft
Weight: average 440 lb; up to 1430 lb

Most familiar to the public through aquariums, TV shows and various celebrity endorsements, the bottlenose dolphin is intelligent and one of the most highly studied cetaceans by marine biologists and behavioral ecologists. Social, behavioral and physical differences between inshore and offshore populations are being studied; in California, local conservation organizations have been photo-identifying the inshore bottlenose dolphin population, which is now estimated to be around 450 individuals. • Markings on the skin and dorsal fins are as distinctive and personal as a fingerprint. **Where found:** inshore and offshore waters all along the coast.

Short-beaked Common Dolphin

Delphinus delphis

Length: average 6½ ft; up to 8½ ft
Weight: average 170 lb; up to 300 lb

Brilliant acrobatics accompany the thrill of having a group of common dolphins swim alongside your boat. They love to bow-ride (riding the momentum of the current made under the bow of a swift-moving boat) and can occur in very large groups of 50–1000 individuals. • The long-beaked common dolphin (*D. capensis*) is very similar both physically and behaviorally to the short-beaked, but a trained eye can observe the characteristic distinctions. **Where found:** offshore along the coast.

Risso's Dolphin

Grampus griseus

Length: average 10 ft; up to 13 ft
Weight: average 880 lb; up to 1100 lb

Risso's dolphins have an interesting social behavior of scratching and biting at each other, leaving white scars all over their bodies—old individuals become so scarred that they appear almost completely white. They can also become scarred from being stung by large squid, their preferred prey. • Off our shores, they are typically observed as solitary individuals or in pairs, but they can occur in large herds, from 25 to several hundred. These dolphins can become quite engaged in play sessions of breaching, spy-hopping, lob-tailing and flipper and fluke slapping. **Where found:** deep, offshore waters.

Northern Elephant Seal

Mirounga angustirostris

Length: *Male:* 12–16 ft; *Female:* 7–12 ft
Weight: *Male:* up to 5070 lb; *Female:* 2000 lb

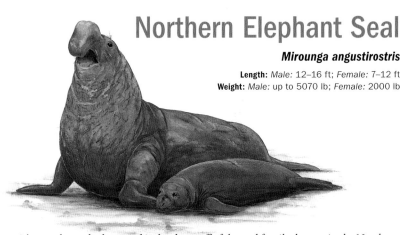

The northern elephant seal is the show-off of the seal family: largest in the Northern Hemisphere, deepest diving (up to 5000 ft) and farthest migrating (up to 13,000 mi). • Between December and March, certain sandy beaches in California become molting, breeding and calving grounds and, consequentially, very noisy and smelly. • Both sexes sport the large snout, but that of the adult male is a pendulous, inflatable (for producing impressive rattling snorts), foot-long "trunk" analogous to its common namesake. **Where found:** sandy beaches during molting, mating and calving.

Harbor Seal

Phoca vitulina

Length: 4–6 ft (tail 3½–4½ in)
Weight: 110–310 lb

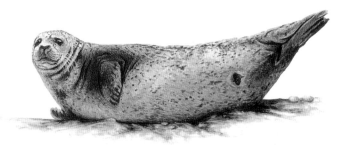

Year round, great colonies of harbor seals can be observed either basking in the day or sleeping at night on rocky shores and islands. Oftentimes during the day, individuals can be seen bobbing vertically in the water—the harbor seal cannot sleep at the surface in the manner in which sea otters can, but it can actually sleep underwater, going without breathing for up to 30 minutes. • These seals are shy of humans but do occasionally pop their heads up beside a canoe or kayak to investigate, then make a quick retreat. **Where found:** bays and estuaries, intertidal sandbars and rocky shorelines along the entire coast of California.

California Sea-Lion

Zalophus californianus

Length: *Male:* 6½–8 ft; *Female:* 4½–6½ ft
Weight: *Male:* 440–860 lb; *Female:* 100–250 lb

If you spend any time on the water off
the coast of California, you are
likely to encounter a California sea-lion or two.
They lounge about on
large buoys, frequent
marinas, pop up
alongside canoe-
ists and kayakers
and swim up to
divers and surfers.
Californian sea-lions
are non-aggressive, often
playful and quite intelligent, as shown by their ability to learn and perform an
array of tricks and stunts in captivity. • The northern (or Steller) sea-lion (*Eume-topias jubatus*) is the only other sea-lion in these waters but is infrequently
observed. **Where found:** in coastal waters, around islands and on rocky or sandy
beaches and floating offshore buoys.

Sea Otter

Enhydra lutris

Length: 2½–5½ ft (tail 10–16 in)
Weight: 50–100 lb

This buoyant otter lolls about on its
back like a sunbather, floating in a manner us humans can only somewhat achieve
in the saltiest of seas. It can even sleep on the water after anchoring itself in kelp
beds, which are habitat for sea urchins, this otter's favored prey. Reluctant to
abandon the comfortable recline, the sea otter grooms itself and dines while floating on its back using tools such as rocks to crack open the shells of its prey. **Where
found:** almost always in the water; shallow, coastal areas with abundant kelp beds;
scattered populations along the coast, with a stable population at San Francisco
Bay, where there is a recovery program.

Northern River Otter

Lutra canadensis

Length: 3½–4½ ft (tail 12–20 in)
Weight: 10–24 lb

The favorite sport of these frisky otters is sliding down wet, grassy riverbanks, even on snowy slopes in winter—look for their slide marks on the banks of rivers, lakes and ponds. • When they are not at play, they are engaged in the business of the hunt. These swift swimmers prey mainly upon aquatic species such as crustaceans, turtles, frogs and fish, but occasionally depredate birds nests and eat small rodents. **Where found:** freshwater and saltwater habitats; lakes, ponds and streams and along the coast.

Fisher

Martes pennanti

Length: 2½–4 ft (tail 12–16 in)
Weight: 4½–12 lb

Despite the name, fishers rarely eat fish but prey upon rodents, hares and birds and also eat berries, nuts and sometimes carrion. They will eat any animal they can overpower, but they are distinguished, along with mountain lions, for their ability to prey upon porcupines. • Fishers are extremely sensitive to any human disturbance and exist only in remote, forested wilderness, where they are a top predator, quickly and nimbly maneuvering throughout the dense habitat. **Where found:** dense mixed and coniferous forests, except redwood forests, through the Cascades and Sierra Nevada and east through the Rockies.

American Marten

Martes americana

Length: 20–26 in (tail 7–9 in)
Weight: 1–3 lb

An expert climber with semi-retractable claws, this forest dweller is quick and agile enough to catch arboreal squirrels such as the red squirrel. Although it spends most of its time on the ground, the marten often dens in a tree-hollow, where it raises its annual litter of 1–5 kits. • Most people only see a marten in the form of a fur stole—the animal is very elusive but not wary enough of the trapline, an ongoing threat even today. To see a marten in the deep forest is to know that you are in true wilderness. **Where found:** old-growth coniferous forests of spruce and fir. **Also known as:** American sable, pine marten.

Short-tailed Weasel

Mustela erminea

Length: 8½–13 in (tail 1½–3½ in)
Weight: 1½–4 oz

Although relatively common, the short-tailed weasel will not
linger for any admiring observers; a spontaneous encounter with this curious creature will reveal its extraordinary
speed and agility as it quickly escapes from view. Its coat
is white in winter, but the tail is black-tipped year
round. • The short-tailed weasel is a voracious nocturnal hunter of mice and voles. **Where found:** dense mixed
and coniferous forests and streamside woodlands; throughout the Sierra Nevada,
Klamath and North Coast mountain ranges. **Also known as:** ermine, stoat.

Long-tailed Weasel

Mustela frenata

Length: 11–16½ in (tail 4½–11½ in)
Weight: 3–14 oz

Following the tracks of the long-tailed weasel on
a snow-covered meadow offers good insight into the
curious and energetic nature of this animal. Seemingly dis-
tracted from walking in a straight line, it continuously zigs and zags to investigate
everything that catches its attention. • The long-tailed weasel feeds on small
rodents, birds, insects, reptiles, amphibians and, occasionally, fruits and berries.
Like other true weasels, it turns white in winter, but the tip of the tail remains
black. **Where found:** aspen parklands, intermontane valleys and open forests.

American Mink

Mustela vison

Length: 18–28 in (tail 5–8½ in)
Weight: 1–3 lb

The mink's partially webbed
feet make it an excellent
swimmer, and it is capable
of diving down to 10 ft in pursuit of fish. Its thick, dark brown to blackish, oily fur
insulates its body from extremely cold water. • Mink travel along established
hunting routes, often along shorelines, rarely passing a prey opportunity and
stashing any surplus kills in temporary dens that are typically dug into riverbanks, beneath rock piles or in evacuated muskrat lodges. **Where found:** shorelines
of lakes, marshes and streams; forests and grasslands in the foothills.

Wolverine

Gulo gulo

Length: 28–43 in (tail 7–10 in)
Weight: 15–35 lb

California's largest member of the weasel family, the wolverine looks like a small, frazzled bear. It has a poor reputation because of its occasional habit of raiding unoccupied wilderness cabins, eating the edible contents and spraying any left-overs with a foul-smelling musk from its anal musk gland...plenty of incentive to lock your cabin tight! • Its wild prey includes marmots, ground squirrels, gophers, mice, insects and berries, and it will scavenge carrion. **Where found:** remote, wooded foothills and montane coniferous forests in the high Sierra Nevada. *Summer:* forages in the alpine tundra and hunts along the slopes. *Winter:* moves to lower elevations. **Also known as:** glutton, skunk bear.

Badger

Taxidea taxus

Length: 25–35 in (tail 5–6½ in)
Weight: 11–24 lb

Equipped with huge claws and strong fore-limbs, the badger is an efficient digger, able to route out a den up to 30 ft long. Once the badger moves its home, these dens are essential in providing den sites, shelters and hibernacula for many creatures, from coyotes to black widow spiders. • The badger's powerful jaws, long teeth and aggressive defense tactics make it a formidable fighter against most predators. It preys almost exclusively upon ground squirrels and other rodents. **Where found:** low-elevation fields, meadows and grasslands; fence lines and ditches.

Striped Skunk

Mephitis mephitis

Length: 22–32 in (tail 8–14 in)
Weight: 4–9½ lb

Only the great horned owl, a regular predator of this small mammal, is undeterred by the odor of the striped skunk. Butylmercaptan is responsible for the stink of the skunk's musk, which is sprayed in defense. If sprayed into the eyes of the skunk's perceived attacker, it can also cause burning, tearing and even temporary blindness. • When undisturbed, the striped skunk is a quiet, reclusive omnivore, feeding on insects, worms, bird eggs, reptiles and amphibians, vegetation and, rarely, small mammals and carrion. **Where found:** lower-elevation streamside woodlands, groves of hardwood trees, semi-open areas, brushy grasslands and valleys; can occur in urban environments, where it will raid gardens and garbage bins.

Western Spotted Skunk

Spilogale gracilis

Length: 13–23 in (tail 4–8 in)
Weight: 1–2 lb

When threatened, this skunk stamps its feet or makes short lunges at its perceived attacker, which will pay the smelly price if it ignores the warning. Although this assault is no laughing matter, the posture this small mammal assumes in order to spray is comical—the skunk literally performs a handstand, arches its back so that its backside and tail face forward above its head, and then walks toward its assailant while spraying. • When not performing such feats of showmanship, this nocturnal skunk feeds on insects, primarily grasshoppers and crickets, but will forage opportunistically for any food source. **Where found:** woodlands, riparian zones, rocky areas, open grasslands or scrublands and farmlands.

Ringtail

Bassariscus astutus

Length: 25–32 in (tail 12–17 in)
Weight: 1½–2½ lb

A member of the raccoon family, the ringtail is reminiscent of a cat, even in the way it hunts by stalking and pouncing upon its prey of small mammals, reptiles and amphibians. The ringtail's omnivorous diet also includes insects, bird eggs and nestlings, carrion and fruit. • Cacomistle, an alternate name for this animal, is derived from the language of the Mexican Nahuatl people and means "half mountain lion," furthering the cat comparisons. Its bushy, ringed tail and its affinity to water associates it to its raccoon kin. **Where found:** rocky slopes and valleys in the foothills; close to water. **Also known as:** cacomistle, civet cat, miner's cat, ring-tailed cat.

Raccoon

Procyon lotor

Length: 26–38 in (tail 7½–16 in)
Weight: 12–31 lb

A garbage container is no match for the raccoon's curiosity, persistence and problem-solving abilities, making your trash and the garden goldfish pond prime targets for midnight food raids in urban areas. In this animal's natural habitat of forest streams, lakes and ponds, an omnivorous diet of clams, frogs, fish, bird eggs and nestlings, berries, nuts and insects is more than ample. Raccoons build up their fat reserves during the warm months to sustain themselves throughout winter. **Where found:** lower-elevation riparian areas; edges of forests and wetlands.

Porcupine

Erethizon dorsatum

Length: 21–37 in (tail 5½–9 in)
Weight: 8–40 lb

A porcupine cannot throw its 30,000 or so quills but delivers them into the flesh of an attacker with a quick flick of the tail. The quills are dangerous but attractive, common in traditional Native American beadwork. • This excellent tree climber fills its vegetarian diet with forbs, shrubs and the sugary cambium of trees. An insatiable craving for salt occasionally drives it to gnaw on rubber tires, wooden ax handles, hiking boots and even toilet seats! • A slow-moving, nocturnal creature, the porcupine is a common roadkill victim. **Where found:** coniferous and mixed forests, open tundra and even rangelands.

Mountain Beaver

Aplodontia rufa

Length: 12–18 in (tail ½–2 in)
Weight: ½–3 lb

Capable of swimming only short distances, this rodent prefers to climb trees, and rather than build an aquatic den, it burrows tunnels and nesting chambers into dry ground. • The mountain beaver feeds primarily on sword ferns and bracken ferns, which are toxic to most other rodents, but also forages on seedlings and the cambium of saplings; the male eats large amounts of red alder leaves in fall. **Where found:** deciduous forests with plenty of shrubs, forbs and young trees; from near sea level to the treeline; northwestern portion of the state to southeast of San Francisco and near the Nevada-California border to the Sierra Nevada.

Beaver

Castor canadensis

Length: 3–4 ft (tail 11–21 in)
Weight: 35–66 lb

The loud slap of a beaver's tail on water warns of intruders. A beaver can remain submerged under water for 15 minutes, and its tail is an extremely effective propulsion device for swimming and diving. • Beavers are skillful and unrelenting in the construction and maintenance of their dams and lodges. They use their long, continuously growing incisors to cut down trees in short order, and their strong jaws can drag a 20-lb piece of wood. **Where found:** lakes, ponds, marshes and slow-flowing rivers and streams at most elevations with ample vegetation.

Common Muskrat

Ondatra zibethicus

Length: 18–24 in (tail 7½–11 in)
Weight: 1½–3½ lb

Although they have similar habitats and behaviors, the beaver and the common muskrat are not closely related. The muskrat does sport large incisors that it uses to cut through a vast array of thick vegetation, particularly cattails and bulrushes, and it makes a partially submerged den similar to that of a beaver, which provides nesting spots for many geese and ducks as well as important shelter for other rodents when the muskrat moves house. **Where found:** low-elevation sloughs, lakes, marshes and streams with plenty of cattails, rushes and open water.

Bushy-tailed Woodrat

Neotoma cinerea

Length: 11–18 in (tail 4½–9 in)
Weight: 3–18 oz

Woodrats are infamous for collecting objects, whether natural or human-made, useful or merely decorative, to add to their large, messy nests. Twigs, bones, pinecones, bottle caps, rings, pens and coins are picked up as this rodent scouts for treasures, often trading an object in its mouth for the next, more attractive item it encounters. A woodrat's nest is often more easily found than the woodrat itself. **Where found:** rocky outcroppings, shrublands, mine shafts and caves; from grasslands to alpine zones. **Also known as:** packrat, trade rat.

Deer Mouse

Peromyscus maniculatus

Length: 5½–8½ in (tail 2–4 in)
Weight: ¾–1¼ oz

Abundant deer mice are seed eaters, but they will also eat insects, spiders, caterpillars, fungi, flowers and berries. Deer mice are in turn important prey for many other animals; thus they must be prolific breeders to maintain their population. A litter of 4–9 young leaves the nest after 3–5 weeks, and the mice are sexually mature 1–2 weeks later. Less than 5% survive a complete year. **Where found:** most dry habitats; grasslands, shrublands and forests; also find ample shelter and food in human settings.

California Vole

Microtus californicus

Length: 6–8½ in (tail 1½–2½ in)
Weight: 1½–3½ oz

There are many species of vole in Northern California, occupying various habitats and ranges. The best way to encounter a vole is to walk through a grassy field and move aside a large piece of debris, such as an abandoned piece of farm equipment or a fallen log. There will probably be a rapid scattering of little mammals, likely voles. **Where found:** grasslands, grassy slopes, saltwater or freshwater marshes and moist meadows; various habitats and elevations throughout the western half of California.

California Kangaroo Rat

Dipodomys californicus

Length: 10–14 in (tail 6–8½ in)
Weight: 1½–2 oz

Named for its manner of hopping on its long-footed hind legs, with its short forelegs held in front like arms, the California kangaroo rat actively hops about most evenings in search of food—mainly seeds and berries, and green vegetation in spring and summer. • Its subterranean burrows have various chambers for nesting, sleeping and storing food as well as several escape tunnels. **Where found:** desert, scrublands and chaparral regions with well-drained soil.

Botta's Pocket Gopher

Thomomys bottae

Length: 6½–11 in (tail 1½–4 in)
Weight: 2½–9 oz

Although rarely seen in a positive light by most farmers and ranchers, pocket gophers are extremely important in natural areas for their practice of turning up large volumes of soil, thus aerating the ground, cycling soil nutrients and improving water absorption, which improves the growth of plants and reduces the takeover of weedy species. • Pocket gophers' subterranean diet comprises mainly roots and tubers. **Where found:** a variety of habitats and soil types, from deserts to mountain meadows; west-central California.

California Ground Squirrel

Spermophilus beecheyi

Length: 14–20 in (tail 5½–8 in)
Weight: 10–26 oz

Although they excavate large burrows that range from 5–200 ft
long, typically under a log, tree
or large boulder, California
ground squirrels are also able to climb 20 ft up a cottonwood tree. • They are non-
colonial but will tolerate being part of loose adult colonies, avoiding the living
spaces of their neighbors. At 8 weeks of age, the young begin to venture away from
the nest and dig their own burrows. **Where found:** open areas; pastures, rocky
outcroppings and rolling hills.

Yellow-bellied Marmot

Marmota flaviventris

Length: 19–26 in (tail 5–7½ in)
Weight: 3½–10 lb

Yellow-bellied marmots live in colonies and excavate a network
of burrows under the rocky terrain to find shelter from the elements and from predators such as eagles or foxes. A loud
chirp of varying intensities alerts the colony to impending
dangers. • Marmots spend their lazy days eating, sleeping and seasonally raising young, basking in the sun on
warm summer days and hibernating in winter. **Where
found:** rocky talus slopes and outcroppings close to a source
of grassy or herbaceous vegetation. **Also known as:** rockchuck.

Yellow-pine Chipmunk

Tamias amoenus

Length: 7½–9½ in (tail 3–4½ in)
Weight: 1½–3 oz

A scurry in the leaf litter in ponderosa pine (also
called yellow pine) forest is likely to be
made by this fidgety chipmunk in
its quest for food: seeds, nuts,
berries, grasses, mushrooms,
insects and sometimes birds'
eggs and nestlings. Once found, the treasure is not necessarily eaten; instead, the
chipmunk's next obsession is to get its food buried in a suitable hiding place in
the ground. **Where found:** open, coniferous forests, sagebrush flats, rocky outcroppings and shrubby pastures; mainly in the north and eastern parts of the state.

67

Western Gray Squirrel

Sciurus griseus

Length: 18–25 in (tail 9½–12 in)
Weight: 1–2 lb

In true squirrel custom, western gray squirrels are so nuts about nuts—acorns, hazelnuts, pine nuts—that they store them in forked tree branches, under fallen logs or underground, where they often germinate, making this squirrel a fortuitous gardener. • Also common in the coniferous coastal rainforest and the Sierra-Cascade forests, Douglas's squirrel (*Tamiasciurus douglasii*), or chickaree, is a brown squirrel with bright orange eye rings and undersides. **Where found:** humid deciduous forests throughout the West Coast and mixed coniferous and oak forests in the Sierra Nevada, Cascade and Klamath ranges. **Also known as:** California gray squirrel, Columbian gray squirrel, silver gray squirrel.

Northern Flying Squirrel

Glaucomys sabrinus

Length: 9½–15 in (tail 4–7 in)
Weight: 2½–6½ oz

Long flaps of skin stretched between the fore and hind limbs and a broad, flattened tail allow the nocturnal northern flying squirrel to glide swiftly from tree to tree, with extreme glides of up to 110 yards! • This flying squirrel plays an important role in forest ecology because it digs up and eats truffles, the fruiting body of a special ectomycorrhizal fungus that grows underground. Through its stool, the squirrel spreads the beneficial fungus, helping both the fungus and the forest plants. **Where found:** primarily old-growth coniferous and mixed forests of the Sierra Nevada, Cascade and Klamath ranges.

Snowshoe Hare

Lepus americanus

Length: 15–21 in (tail 2 in)
Weight: 2–3½ lb

Extremely well adapted to surviving harsh alpine winters, the snowshoe hare has large hind feet that allow it to move across deep snow without sinking in, and the white pelage in winter camouflages it. If detected by a predator, the hare explodes into a running zig-zag pattern in its flight for cover, sometimes reaching speeds of 32 mph. • Populations of the snowshoe hare, its winter food sources of willow and alder and its main predator, the lynx, are closely inter-related and cyclical. **Where found:** brushy, second-growth forests; throughout most of the Sierra-Cascade ranges. **Also known as:** varying hare.

Black-tailed Jackrabbit

Lepus californicus

Length: 20–24 in (tail 2½–4 in)
Weight: 5–10 lb

This hare can often be seen at dawn and dusk grazing at roadsides. Although it can run up to 35 mph and leap as far as 20 ft when frightened, the black-tailed jackrabbit still falls prey to eagles, hawks, owls, coyotes and bobcats. • It does not turn white in winter like its cousin, the white-tailed jackrabbit (*L. townsendii*), found east of the Sierra-Cascade ranges. **Where found:** lower-elevation shrublands, sagebrush, fields and grasslands; from the foothills to the coast.

Pygmy Rabbit

Brachylagus idahoensis

Length: 10–12 in (tail 1–1½ in)
Weight: 10–15 oz

This tiny, native rabbit has a very limited northeastern range in California, overlapping slightly with the mountain cottontail but favoring desert or semi-desert conditions. It is a keystone species in these habitats and is unable to survive elsewhere. Many other species are dependent upon its presence as prey or for use of its abandoned burrows. • Bitter sagebrush leaves are the major component of this rabbit's diet. **Where found:** dense stands of sagebrush or rabbitbrush in desert and semi-desert areas of northeastern California.

Brush Rabbit

Sylvilagus bachmani

Length: 11–15 in (tail ½–1½ in)
Weight: 1–2 lb

This tiny rabbit is commonly seen wherever there is some nearby brush for shelter and tender vegetation for food. It is typically active at dawn and dusk. • Females are capable of up to 5 litters of 3–4 young per litter in a single year. • The 3 *Sylvilagus* species in California are similar in appearance but have different ranges, though the brush rabbit and the desert cottontail do overlap. **Where found:** areas with plenty of brush cover; all along the lower elevation zones of the western region of the state.

Mountain Cottontail

Sylvilagus nuttallii

Length: 13–16 in (tail 1–2½ in)
Weight: 1½–2½ lb

Mountain cottontails hide out during the day in shallow burrows, called forms, covered by impenetrable vegetation, or they hide in rock crevices. Their secretive nature is owing to their many predators, which include bobcats, coyotes and birds of prey. As well, the adults do not camouflage white in winter; thus, they become even more reclusive but do not hibernate. **Where found:** sagebrush, rocky areas interspersed with shrubs and riparian areas; east of the Sierra-Cascades and on the Modoc Plateau. **Also known as:** Nuttall's cottontail (named after early-19th-century explorer and naturalist Thomas Nuttall).

Pika

Ochotona princeps

Length: 6½–8½ in
Weight: 4–6½ oz

The busy pika scurries in and out of rocky crevices to issue its warning *PEEEK!* call and to gather large bundles of succulent grasses to dry on sun-drenched rocks and store for later consumption during winter, when they rarely leave their shelters under the snow. In summer, they make grassy nests within the rocks to have their young. • Although tail-less and with rounded ears, the pika is a close relative of rabbits and hares. **Where found:** rocky talus slopes and rocky fields at higher elevations. **Also known as:** cony.

Brazilian Free-tailed Bat

Tadarida brasiliensis

Length: 3½–4½ in (tail 1–2 in)
Wingspan: 11 in (forearm 1½–2 in)
Weight: ¼–½ oz

Brazilian free-tailed bats have impressively large colony sizes, and they vacate their roosts at night in overwhelming numbers. One of the most famous such colonies is in the Carlsbad Caverns of New Mexico, which has a population millions strong. Although not in such great numbers in California, they still are seen exiting caves *en masse*, and large colonies can blanket the ceilings of caves and mines; nursing colonies can have as many as 1500 pups per square foot! **Where found:** crevices, tunnels, mines, caves and vacated buildings; pinyon-juniper forests of the north. **Also known as:** guano bat.

Western Mastiff Bat

Eumops perotis

Length: 5½–7½ in (tail 1½–3 in)
Wingspan: 20–23 in (forearm 3 in)
Weight: 2¼ oz

This free-tailed bat is the largest in North America. Commonly referred to as the mastiff bat for its pushed-in, pug-like face, which resembles that of a mastiff, this bat actually has quite a delicate face, if you should ever get a close look. • Its lengthy feeding forays, up to 6–7 hours, might be attributed to its finicky eating habits; this bat plucks the wings, heads and legs off insects before eating them. **Where found:** arid regions with rocky sites or cliffs for roosting; may occur in semi-arid open woodlands; only as far north as the San Francisco Bay area in the Coast Mountains and equally far north in the Sierra Nevada.

Little Brown Bat

Myotis lucifugus

Length: 2½–4 in (tail 1–2 in)
Wingspan: 10 in (forearm 1½ in)
Weight: ¼ oz

These common bats form large maternal roosting colonies each summer to give birth and raise young and are frequently seen flying at night in pursuit of insects or skimming over water sources such as lakes and ponds, even swimming pools, to get a quick drink. • All the mouse-eared bats (*Myotis* spp.) are generally indistinguishable as they fly in dim light. **Where found:** various habitats and elevations; roosts in buildings, barns, caves, rock crevices, hollow trees and under tree bark; hibernates in buildings, caves and mine adits.

Hoary Bat

Lasiurus cinereus

Length: 4–6 in (tail 1½–2½ in)
Wingspan: 16 in (forearm 1¾–2¼ in)
Weight: 1–1¼ oz

This large, beautiful bat roosts in trees, not caves or buildings, and wraps its wings around itself for protection against the elements, its frosty-colored fur blending in amongst the mosses and lichens. The hoary bat also roosts in orchards, but it is an insectivore and does not damage fruit crops. At night, look for its large size and slow wingbeats over open terrain. **Where found:** roosts on the branches of coniferous and deciduous trees and occasionally in tree cavities.

Western Pipistrelle

Pipistrellus hesperus

Length: 2½–3½ in (tail 1–1¼ in)
Wingspan: 7½–8½ in (forearm 1–1¼ in)
Weight: up to ¼ oz

This is the smallest bat in the U.S. It is also quite delicate, with a weak, erratic flight style, making it unable to fly in strong wind. The jerky flight of its European counterparts gave it the name "flittermouse" (or *fledermaus* in German). • The contrasting black mask, wings and legs against blond fur make this bat distinctively attractive. **Where found:** arid regions with rocky or scrubby areas, sometimes close to cities; only as far north as the upper San Joaquin Valley and San Francisco Bay area.

Silver-haired Bat

Lasionycteris noctivagans

Length: 3½–4½ in (tail 1½–2 in)
Wingspan: 12 in (forearm 1½–2 in)
Weight: ¼–½ oz

Silver-haired bats take flight at dawn and dusk on feeding forays for moths, flying over open fields, water surfaces and treetops. • To conserve energy on cold days, they can lower their body temperature and metabolism and go into a state known as torpor. • These bats prefer to roost in trees. Small colonies of silver-haired bats may choose to hibernate in caves, mines or abandoned buildings. Females form nursery colonies in protected shelters such as tree cavities. **Where found:** roosts in cavities and crevices of old-growth trees but can adapt to parks, cities and farmlands.

Big Brown Bat

Eptesicus fuscus

Length: 3½–5½ in (tail 1–2½ in)
Wingspan: 13 in (forearm 1½–2 in)
Weight: ½–1 oz

An effective aerial hunter, the big brown bat's ultrasonic echolocation (80,000–40,000 Hz) can detect flying insects up to 16 ft away. It flies above water, around street lights or over agricultural areas hunting insects at dusk and dawn. • The big brown bat is not abundant but is frequently encountered because of its tendency to roost in human-made structures. It has been known to change hibernation sites in midwinter, a time when it is extremely rare to spot a bat. **Where found:** in and around human-made structures; occasionally roosts in hollow trees and rock crevices.

Pallid Bat

Antrozous pallidus

Length: 3½–5½ in (tail 1½–2 in)
Wingspan: 15 in (forearm 2–2½ in)
Weight: ½–1¼ oz

The pallid bat is known to grab the occasional insect or other invertebrate from the ground, which is unusual and risky behavior. The bat is vulnerable prey itself when on the ground, whereas there are few predators in the night sky. • The pallid bat often has separate night and day roosting sites: caves, overhangs or buildings at night and buildings or rock crevices by day. **Where found:** rocky outcrops near open, dry areas; occasionally evergreen forests; throughout Northern California except the northwestern Klamath and Siskiyou mountain zones.

Townsend's Big-eared Bat

Plecotus townsendii

Length: 3½–4½ in (tail 1–2½ in)
Wingspan: 11 in (forearm 1½–2 in)
Weight: ¼–½ oz

Endowed with relatively enormous ears, these bats "see" the nighttime world through sound (though all bats have good eyesight, contrary to the blind-as-a-bat myth). Each species of bat is recognizable by the ultrasonic calls it produces, but special equipment is needed to identify bat calls. They can hear frequencies as much as 200 times higher than our ears can hear. **Where found:** open areas near coniferous forests; hibernate deep within caves. **Also known as:** western big-eared bat.

Broad-footed Mole

Scapanus latimanus

Length: 5–7½ in (tail 1–2 in)
Weight: 2 oz

With little use for eyesight in a life spent underground, the nearly blind broad-footed mole has a sensitive tail and long snout that "see" by feeling as this little mammal burrows through the earth with its strong, paddle-like feet endowed with long, dirt-digging claws. • Another intriguing adaptation to its lifestyle is the mole's velvety fur, which lies flat forward and backward facing, permitting the animal to move in either direction without resistance. **Where found:** soft, moist soils at various elevations throughout Northern California.

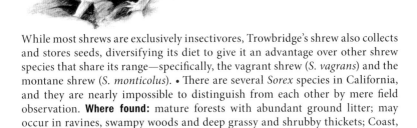

Trowbridge's Shrew

Sorex trowbridgii

Length: 4–5½ in (tail 2–2½ in)
Weight: ¼ oz

While most shrews are exclusively insectivores, Trowbridge's shrew also collects and stores seeds, diversifying its diet to give it an advantage over other shrew species that share its range—specifically, the vagrant shrew (*S. vagrans*) and the montane shrew (*S. monticolus*). • There are several *Sorex* species in California, and they are nearly impossible to distinguish from each other by mere field observation. **Where found:** mature forests with abundant ground litter; may occur in ravines, swampy woods and deep grassy and shrubby thickets; Coast, Klamath, Cascade and Sierra Nevada ranges.

Virginia Opossum

Didelphis virginiana

Length: 27–33 in (tail 12–14 in)
Weight: 2½–3½ lb

Contrary to most children's stories in which opossums are portrayed hanging by their prehensile tails, the Virginia opossum rarely assumes this posture, though it does climb and den in trees. It is a marsupial closely related to kangaroos and koalas. • The trick of playing dead, a role this actor is famous for, is performed when attacked in hopes of being left alone. This is where the expression "playing possum" comes from. However, playing dead has unsuccessful results against cars, which are this slow-moving nocturnal creature's most common assailant. **Where found:** moist woodlands or brushy areas near watercourses; northwestern portion of the state.

BIRDS

All birds are feathered but not all fly. The most diverse class of vertebrates, birds are bipedal, warm-blooded and lay hard-shelled eggs. Some birds migrate south in the colder winter months and return north in spring. For this reason, Northern California has a different diversity of birds in summer than in winter. Many migrating birds fly as far south as Central and South America. These neotropical migrants are of concern to biologists and conservationists because pesticide use and decreasing habitat in these countries threaten the survival of many species. Education and increasing appreciation for wildlife may encourage solutions to this problem.

Waterfowl
pp. 77–81

Grouse-like Birds
pp. 81–82

Diving Birds
pp. 83–84

Herons & Vultures
pp. 85–86

Birds of Prey
pp. 87–90

Rails & Coots
pp. 90–91

Shorebirds
pp. 91–93

Gulls, Terns & Alcids
pp. 93–95

Pigeons & Doves
pp. 95–96

Owls
pp. 96–97

Swifts
p. 97

Hummingbirds &
Kingfishers, pp. 97–98

Woodpeckers
pp. 98–100

Flycatchers
pp. 100–01

Shrikes & Vireos
pp. 101–02

Jays & Crows
pp. 102–03

Larks & Swallows
p. 104

Chickadees & Nuthatches
pp. 105–06

Wrens & Kinglets
p. 106

Thrushes
p. 107

**Wrentits, Starlings &
Waxwings,** p. 108

Wood-warblers & Tanagers
pp. 109–10

Sparrows & Grosbeaks
pp. 110–12

Blackbirds & Allies
pp. 112–13

Finch-like Birds
pp. 114–15

Canada Goose

Branta canadensis

Length: 35–45 in
Wingspan: 4½–6 ft

Canada geese mate for life and are devoted parents to their 2–11 goslings. Wild geese can be aggressive when defending young or competing for food. Hissing sounds and low, outstretched necks are signs that you should give these birds some space. • Geese graze on aquatic grasses and sprouts, and you can spot them tipping up to grab for aquatic roots and tubers. • The Canada goose was split into 2 species in 2004; the smaller subspecies have been renamed the "cackling goose." **Where found:** along waterbodies; parks, marshes and croplands.

Mallard

Anas platyrhynchos

Length: 20–28 in
Wingspan: 3 ft

The male mallard, with his shiny, green head and chestnut brown breast, is the classic wild duck, and this duck species is one of the only ones that really "quacks." • A grass nest is built on the ground or under a bush, where the female incubates 7–10 creamy, grayish or greenish white eggs. Mallards readily hybridize with a variety of other duck species, including barnyard ducks, often producing offspring with very peculiar plumages. **Where found:** lakes, wetlands, rivers, city parks, agricultural areas, sewage lagoons and even outdoor swimming pools; year round.

Cinnamon Teal

Anas cyanoptera
Length: 15–17 in
Wingspan: 20–22 in

Cinnamon teals push northward each spring from southwestern, middle American wintering grounds to nest in the valleys on both sides of the Sierra-Cascade divide, breeding locally west to the coastal and near-coastal lowlands. They are most common in the alkaline bulrush marshes of the Great Basin and in managed Klamath Basin wetlands. **Where found:** freshwater ponds, marshes, sloughs and flooded swales.

Northern Shoveler

Anas clypeata
Length: 18–20 in
Wingspan: 30 in

An extra large, spoon-like bill allows the northern shoveler to strain small invertebrates from the water and from the bottoms of ponds. This specialized feeding strategy means that it is rarely seen tipping up, but more likely found in the shallows of ponds and marshes where the mucky bottom is easiest to access. **Where found:** shallow marshes, bogs and lakes with muddy bottoms and emergent vegetation; usually in open and semi-open areas.

Lesser Scaup

Aythya affinis

Length: 15–18 in
Wingspan: 25 in

Two scaup species occur in our area, and their tricolor appearance makes these widespread diving ducks easy to recognize and remember. The lesser scaup has a smaller white inner wing stripe visible in flight that becomes dull gray on theprimaries, while the greater scaup (*A. marila*) has a larger white wing stripe that extends into the secondary flight feathers. The male lesser scaup has a purple, peaked head, whereas the greater scaup has a green, rounded head. **Where found:** *Breeding:* large, shallow lakes of the Klamath Basin. *In migration* and *winter:* shallow, fresh and estuarine waters.

Surf Scoter

Somateria perspicillata

Length: 17–21 in
Wingspan: 28–31 in

The surf scoter sits like a sturdy buoy on the waves of bays, inlets and large lakes. This bird breeds in Alaska and northern Canada and is well adapted for life on rough waters, spending winters just beyond the breaking surf on the Atlantic and Pacific coasts. • Although the surf scoter is the only scoter that breeds and overwinters exclusively on this continent, it is largely unstudied. **Where found:** bays and inlets along the coast; large, deep lakes and slow-moving rivers in the interior.

Bufflehead

Bucephala albeola

Length: 13–15 in
Wingspan: 21 in

The typical bufflehead spends its entire life in North America; it has its breeding grounds in the boreal forests of Canada and Alaska and winters primarily in marine bays and estuaries along the Atlantic and Pacific coasts. Many of these ducks migrate through our region, and a few stay on to overwinter on our larger lakes and rivers. • Fish, crustaceans and mollusks make up a major portion of the bufflehead's winter diet, but in summer, this duck eats large amounts of aquatic invertebrates and tubers. **Where found:** open water on lakes, large ponds and rivers.

Common Merganser

Mergus merganser

Length: 22–27 in
Wingspan: 34 in

The common merganser must run along the surface of the water beating its heavy wings to gain sufficient lift to take off; once up and away, it flies arrow-straight and low over the water. • This large duck nests in a tree cavity, on a cliff ledge, in a large nest box or occasionally on the ground, usually close to water. • In winter, any source of open water with a fish-filled shoal will support good numbers of these skilled divers. **Where found:** large rivers and deep lakes.

Ruddy Duck

Owyura jamaicensis

Length: 15–16 in
Wingspan: 18–19 in

The male ruddy duck's red feathers and large, blue bill make this duck eye-catching and unforgettably endearing. With a bill-pumping display followed by staccato grunting as he courts a mate, he further draws our attention. **Where found:** *Breeding:* large, deepwater marshes and the margins of reed-skirted ponds. *Winter:* birds assemble in large flocks on still or protected tidal waters.

Ring-necked Pheasant

Phasianus colchicus

Length: *Male:* 30–36 in; *Female:* 20–26 in
Wingspan: *Male:* 31 in; *Female:* 28 in

Since being introduced in the late 1800s, this Asian bird has had to endure many pressures. Its numbers have had to be continually replenished by hatchery-raised young, not only because it is hunted, but also because of diminished habitat, intensive farming practices and harsh winters. • Unlike native grouse, the ring-necked pheasant lacks feathered legs and feet for insulation. It cannot survive on native plants but depends on grain and corn crops. **Where found:** shrubby grasslands, urban parks, hayfields, grassy ditches and fence lines, woodlots and occasionally croplands; the Sacramento Valley, the San Joaquin Valley and the Modoc Plateau.

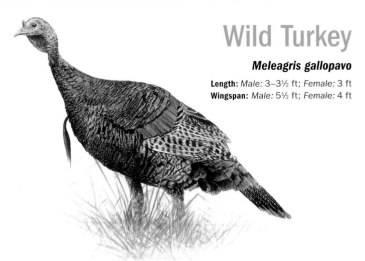

Wild Turkey

Meleagris gallopavo

Length: *Male:* 3–3½ ft; *Female:* 3 ft
Wingspan: *Male:* 5½ ft; *Female:* 4 ft

Wild turkeys were once common throughout most of eastern North America, but habitat loss and over-hunting took a toll on them in the early 20th century. Restoration efforts have reestablished wild turkeys in many areas of our region. • This charismatic bird is the only native North American animal that has been widely domesticated. The wild ancestors of most domestic animals came from Europe. **Where found:** deciduous and mixed oak-conifer forest edges and clearings; riparian woodlands, foothills and lower slopes; occasionally eats waste grain and corn in late fall and winter.

California Quail

Callipepla californica

Length: 10–11 in
Wingspan: 14 in

First introduced to our area in the 1800s, though largely absent from the coast, California quails are year-round residents in low-elevation brushy habitats and parks. They are seen scuttling about in tight, cohesive flocks, sometimes of up to 200 birds. The unmistakeable feature of this bird is the truly cute head plumage. • It typically falls prey to feral cats, but most predatory birds and mammals would make the effort to catch this plump meal. **Where found:** chaparral, brush, suburban parks and oak and riparian woodlands.

Common Loon

Gavia immer

Length: 28–35 in
Wingspan: 4–5 ft

Loons actually have several different calls. A single loon will give a laughing distress call, separated pairs seem to wail *Where aaare you?* and groups give soft, cohesive hoots as they fly. • Most birds have hollow bones, but loons have solid bones, which reduces their buoyancy and enables them to dive to maximum depths of 180 ft. • These birds once summered on lakes in northeastern California, but today, they occur only as migrant and wintering nonbreeders. **Where found:** open water; coastal waters, estuaries, lakes, reservoirs and large rivers.

Pied-billed Grebe

Podilymbus podiceps

Length: 12–15 in
Wingspan: 16 in

Relatively solid bones and the ability to partially deflate its air sac allow the pied-billed grebe to sink below the surface of the water like a tiny submarine. • Although local populations stay year round, on fall evenings, an influx of the migrant populations of these grebes can be seen returning to the ponds, lakes and estuaries where they spend winter. **Where found:** *Breeding:* deep, freshwater lakes, ponds and other water sources. *Nonbreeding:* varied open and semi-open fresh and estuarine waters and kelp beds.

Eared Grebe

Podiceps nigricollis

Length: 11½–14 in
Wingspan: 16 in

Eared grebes undergo cyclical periods of atrophy and hypertrophy of their internal organs and pectoral muscles, depending on whether or not the birds need to migrate. This strategy leaves eared grebes flightless for up to 10 months annually— longer than any other flying bird in the world. • Typically colonial nesters, these grebes make floating platform nests among thick vegetation on the edge of a lake or wetland. **Where found:** *Breeding:* freshwater or slightly alkaline wetlands with floating or emergent vegetation. *Nonbreeding:* coastal waters, lagoons and open estuaries; interior lakes, reservoirs, ponds and slow rivers.

Western Grebe

Aechmophorus occidentalis

Length: 25 in
Wingspan: 24 in

Elegant western grebes are famous for their elaborate courtship rituals, in which pairs caress each other with aquatic vegetation and sprint side by side, literally walking on water. The breeding pair will build a floating nest of wet vegetation anchored to submerged plants and incubate 2–4 eggs. The hatchlings climb directly from the egg onto the parents' backs. **Where found:** *Breeding:* large lakes with dense vegetation. *Nonbreeding:* almost any sizeable body of open water.

Brown Pelican

Pelecanus occidentalis

Length: 48 in
Wingspan: 84 in

With even wing beats, brown pelicans fly gracefully above sunbathers and boaters, but then dive bomb head first with folded wings into the water, to depths of up to 60 ft, to catch fish. • Prior to the 1950s and 1960s, brown pelicans nested north to Point Lobos, Monterey County, but DDT-related reproductive failures caused the population to crash. Now, nearly all the brown pelicans visiting Northern California originate in Mexico. **Where found:** coastal and estuarine waters; visit offshore islands; roosts on protected islets, sea stacks, sandbars and piers.

Double-crested Cormorant

Phalacrocorax auritus

Length: 26–32 in
Wingspan: 4¼ ft

The double-crested cormorant looks like a bird but smells and swims like a fish. With a long, rudder-like tail, excellent underwater vision, sealed nostrils for diving and "wettable" feathers (lacking oil glands), this bird has mastered the underwater world. • Cormorants often perch with their wings partially spread. They are colonial nesters and build their nests on platforms of sticks and guano. • A traditional Japanese fishing method called *Ukai* employs cormorants on leashes to catch fish. **Where found:** large lakes and large, meandering rivers; nests on islands or in trees.

Great Blue Heron

Ardea herodias

Length: 4¼–4½ ft
Wingspan: 6 ft

The long-legged great blue heron employs
a stealthy, often motionless hunting strategy. It waits for a fish or frog to approach,
spears the prey with its bill, then flips its catch
into the air and swallows it whole. Herons usually
hunt near water, but they also stalk fields and meadows in search of rodents.
• Great blue herons settle in communal treetop nests called rookeries, and nest
width can reach 4 ft. **Where found:** forages along edges of rivers, lakes and
marshes; also in fields and meadows.

Great Egret

Ardea alba

Length: 3–3½ ft
Wingspan: 4 ft

The plumes of great egrets and snowy egrets were
widely used to decorate hats in the early 20th century. Some of the first conservation legislation in
North America was enacted to outlaw the hunting of great egrets; the great egret is the symbol
for the National Audubon Society, one of the
oldest conservation organizations in the United States.
Where found: marshes, open riverbanks, irrigation
canals and lakeshores; nests in dense tree stands.

Snowy Egret

Egretta thula

Length: 22–26 in
Wingspan: 3½ ft

Looking as if it stepped in a can of yellow paint, the
dainty snowy egret flaunts famously yellow feet on
black legs. Come breeding season, the egret's lores and
feet turn a deeper orange, and long plumes—perhaps
the most sought-after for the plume trade—extend from
its neck and back. • Snowy egrets teetered on the brink of
extirpation from our region by the early 1900s but have
recovered dramatically and now occur beyond their historical range limits. **Where found:** edges of marshes,
rivers, lakes and ponds; flooded agricultural fields.

85

Turkey Vulture

Cathartes aura

Length: 25–31 in
Wingspan: 5½–6 ft

Turkey vultures are playful and social birds, and groups live and sleep together in large trees, or roosts. Some roost sites are over a century old and have been used by the same family of vultures for several generations. • The genus name *Cathartes* means "cleanser" and refers to this bird's affinity for carrion. • No other bird uses updrafts and thermals in flight as well as the turkey vulture. Pilots have reported seeing vultures soaring at 20,000 ft. **Where found:** usually flies over open country, shorelines or roads; rarely over forests.

California Condor

Gymnogyps californianus

Length: 3½–4½ ft
Wingspan: 8½–9½ ft

The massive California condor has become an emblem of the complexities of wildlife conservation. Once ranging across the country, its decline since the beginning of European settlement is the result of shooting, poisoning, egg collection, nest harassment and food scarcity. The last wild condor went into captivity in 1987, and today, all condors are captive bred and released into uncertain futures. California condors are a marked, radio-tagged and intensely managed remnant species, unable to fulfill any meaningful ecological role today. **Where found:** arid foothills, mountains and canyons; captive-bred birds have been released into the Sespe Condor Sanctuary and Big Sur coast.

Osprey

Pandion haliaetus

Length: 22–25 in
Wingspan: 5½–6 ft

While hunting for fish, the large and powerful osprey hovers in the air before hurling itself in a dramatic headfirst dive. An instant before striking the water, it rights itself and thrusts its feet forward to grasp its quarry. • Ospreys build bulky nests on high, artificial structures such as communication towers and utility poles, or on buoys and channel markers over water, where the pair tends to 2–3 chicks. **Where found:** lakes and slow-flowing rivers and streams. *In migration:* estuaries and bays.

White-tailed Kite

Elanus leucurus

Length: 15–17 in
Wingspan: 3¼ ft

This dedicated hunter seeks prey from early morning until twilight. When it spots a meal, such as a vole scurrying in the grass, it drops to the earth with its wings held high like a parachute. • The white-tailed kite flies with a grace and buoyancy uncommon among raptors. Evening roosts in winter sometimes number over 100 birds. • Formerly known as the "black-shouldered kite," its numbers are now strong in western California after near extirpation from the state in the early 20th century. **Where found:** tree-dotted lowland, hillside fields, non-grazed grasslands and marshes.

Bald Eagle

Haliaeetus leucocephalus

Length: 30–43 in
Wingspan: 5½–8 ft

While soaring hundreds of feet high in the air, bald eagles can spot fish swimming underwater and small rodents scurrying through the grass. • Bald eagles do not mature until their fourth or fifth year. Only then do they develop the characteristic white head and tail plumage. • Bald eagles mate for life and renew pair bonds by adding sticks to their same nests each year, which can be up to 15 ft in diameter—the largest of any North American bird. **Where found:** near large lakes and rivers.

Northern Harrier

Circus cyaneus

Length: 16–24 in
Wingspan: 3½–4 ft

The courtship flight of the northern harrier is a spectacle worth watching in spring. The male climbs almost vertically in the air, then stalls and plummets in a reckless dive toward the ground. At the last second, he saves himself with a hairpin turn that sends him skyward again. • Britain's Royal Air Force named the Harrier aircraft after the northern harrier for its impressive maneuverability. **Where found:** open country; fields, wet meadows, cattail marshes, bogs and croplands; nests on the ground, usually in tall vegetation.

Sharp-shinned Hawk

Accipiter striatus

Length: *Male:* 10–12 in; *Female:* 12–14 in
Wingspan: *Male:* 20–24 in; *Female:* 24–28 in

After a successful hunt, the small sharp-shinned hawk often perches on a favorite "plucking post" with its meal in its razor-sharp talons. This accipiter, or woodland hawk, preys almost exclusively on small birds. • Short, rounded wings, a long, rudder-like tail and flap-and-glide flight allow this hawk to maneuver through the forest at high speed. • As it ages, the sharp-shinned hawk's bright yellow eyes become red. **Where found:** dense to semi-open coniferous forests and large woodlots; occasionally along rivers and in urban areas; may visit backyard bird feeders to prey on feeding sparrows and finches in winter.

Cooper's Hawk

Accipiter cooperii

Length: *Male:* 15–17 in; *Female:* 17–19 in
Wingspan: *Male:* 27–32 in; *Female:* 32–37 in

Cooper's hawk will quickly change the scene at a backyard bird feeder when it comes looking for a meal. European starlings, American robins and house sparrows are among its favorite choices of prey. When there are no feeders in the area, it hunts along forest edges. With the help of its short, square tail and flap-and-glide flight, it is capable of maneuvering quickly at high speeds to snatch its prey in mid-air. **Where found:** mixed and riparian woodlands; urban gardens with feeders; nests in trees, often near a stream or pond.

Red-shouldered Hawk

Buteo lineatus

Length: 19 in
Wingspan: 3½ ft

The red-shouldered hawk nests in mature trees, usually in river bottoms and lowland tracts of woods alongside creeks. As spring approaches and pair bonds are formed, this normally quiet hawk utters loud, shrieking *key-ah* calls. If left undisturbed, red-shouldered hawks will remain faithful to productive nesting sites, returning yearly for generations. **Where found:** mature deciduous and mixed forests, swampy woodlands, coastal bottomlands, agricultural lands, suburbs and city parks, lightly wooded foothills and unmanaged riversides.

Red-tailed Hawk

Buteo jamaicensis

Length: *Male:* 18–23 in; *Female:* 20–25 in
Wingspan: 4–5 ft

Spend a summer afternoon in the country, and you will likely see a red-tailed hawk perched on a fence post or soaring on thermals. • Courting red-tails will sometimes dive at one another, lock talons and tumble toward the earth, breaking away at the last second to avoid crashing into the ground. • The red-tailed hawk's piercing call is often paired with the image of an eagle in TV commercials and movies. **Where found:** open country with some trees; also roadsides or woodlots; can often be seen flying above cities.

American Kestrel

Falco sparverius

Length: 7½–8 in
Wingspan: 20–24 in

The colorful American kestrel, formerly known as the "sparrow hawk," is a common and widespread bird, not shy of human activity and adaptable to habitat change. This small falcon has benefited from the grassy rights-of-way created by interstate highways. They provide habitat for grasshoppers, which make up most of its diet, as well as other small prey such as mice. **Where found:** along rural roadways, perched on poles and telephone wires; agricultural and open fields, grasslands, riparian woodlands, woodlots, forest edges, bogs, roadside ditches and grassy highway medians.

Peregrine Falcon

Falco peregrinus

Length: *Male:* 15–17 in; *Female:* 17–19 in
Wingspan: Male: 3–3½ ft; Female: 3½–4 ft

Nothing causes more panic in a flock of ducks or shore-birds than a hunting peregrine falcon. This agile raptor matches every twist and turn the flock makes, then dives to strike a lethal blow. • The peregrine falcon is the world's fastest bird. In a headfirst dive, it can reach speeds of up to 220 mph. • Peregrine falcons represent a successful conservation effort since the banning of DDT in North America in 1972. **Where found:** lakeshores, river valleys, river mouths, urban areas and open fields; nests on rocky cliffs or skyscraper ledges.

Virginia Rail

Rallus limicola

Length: 9–11 in
Wingspan: 13 in

Sit along any wetland marsh and clap your hands a few times—a Virginia rail may peek out of the vegetation for a moment, but more likely it will respond with a telegraph-like clicking call. • The Virginia rail and its relative, the sora (similar in shape but with a short bill), often successfully coexist in the same marshes: the Virginia rail favors dry shores of marshes and feeds on invertebrates; the sora (*Porzana carolina*) prefers waterfront property and eats plants and seeds. **Where found:** wetlands; cattail and bulrush marshes.

Common Moorhen

Gallinula chloropus

Length: 12–15 in
Wingspan: 20–23 in

With the bill of a chicken, the body of a duck and the long legs and large feet of a heron, the common moorhen is comedic to observe. Lacking webbed feet, it is still a capable swimmer and occasional diver. It occupies much of its time strutting about the wetland gleaning the vegetation and preying upon tadpoles, insects, snails, worms and spiders, or building vegetative platforms for nesting, brooding and roosting. **Where found:** large, freshwater marshes with standing water and broken stands of tall, emergent vegetation; year-round resident in the San Joaquin Valley up to the Sacramento Valley; Monterey Bay and San Francisco Bay areas in winter.

American Coot

Fulica americana

Length: 13–16 in
Wingspan: 24 in

This bird's behavior during the breeding season confirms the expression, "crazy as a coot." It is aggressively territorial and constantly squabbles with other water birds in its space. • With feet that have individually webbed toes, the coot is adapted to diving, but it also isn't afraid to steal a meal from another skilled diver when a succulent piece of water celery is brought to the surface. **Where found:** shallow marshes, ponds and wetlands with open water and emergent vegetation; sewage lagoons and inshore kelp beds.

Black-bellied Plover

Pluvialis squatarola

Length: 10½–13 in
Wingspan: 29 in

Black-bellied plovers may be seen along the coast in winter, roosting in tight flocks or running along the mudflats when the tide goes out. These large plovers forage for small invertebrates with a robin-like run-and-stop technique, frequently pausing to lift their heads for a reassuring scan of their surroundings. • Watch for small flocks flashing their bold white wing stripes as they fly low over the water's surface. **Where found:** coastal mudflats and beaches; plowed fields, sod farms and meadows in the San Joaquin Valley; edges of lakeshores and reservoirs.

Killdeer

Charadrius vociferus

Length: 9–11 in
Wingspan: 24 in

The killdeer is a gifted actor, well known for its "broken wing" distraction display. When an intruder wanders too close to its nest (on open ground in a shallow, usually unlined depression), the killdeer greets the interloper with piteous cries while dragging a wing and stumbling about as if injured. Most predators take the bait and follow, and once the killdeer has lured the predator far away from its nest, it miraculously recovers from the injury and flies off with a loud call. **Where found:** open, wet meadows, lakeshores, sandy beaches, mudflats, gravel streambeds and golf courses.

Black-necked Stilt

Himantopus mexicanus

Length: 14–15 in
Wingspan: 29 in

Extraordinarily long, stilt-like legs make this bird an exceptional wader. Proportionally, it has the longest legs of any North American bird. • The black-necked stilt uses its long, needle-like bill to pick insects, crustaceans and other aquatic invertebrates from the water's surface or to probe the substrate for prey. **Where found:** year-round resident in the San Joaquin Valley; throughout summer farther north up the Sacramento Valley to the Modoc Plateau. *Breeding:* along the margins of freshwater, brackish or saltwater marshes; marshy shorelines of lakes, ponds and tidal mudflats.

American Avocet

Recurvirostra americana

Length: 17–18 in
Wingspan: 31 in

An American avocet in full breeding plumage, with a peachy red head and neck, needle-like bill and black and white body, paints an elegant picture against the uniform mudflats. • Females have been known to parasitize the nests of other avocets and perhaps other species. Conversely, avocets have incubated common tern and black-necked stilt eggs, raising the adopted nestlings along with their own young. **Where found:** lakeshores, alkaline wetlands, exposed mudflats, coastal estuaries, shallow lagoons, salt evaporation ponds and shallow, freshwater sloughs and ponds.

Spotted Sandpiper

Actitis macularius

Length: 7–8 in
Wingspan: 15 in

The female spotted sandpiper diligently defends her territory, mates, lays her eggs and leaves the male to tend the clutch. Only about 1% of birds display this unusual breeding strategy known as polyandry. She may mate with several different males, lay up to 4 clutches and produce 20 eggs in a summer. The male then incubates the eggs for 20–24 days, taking on this role because of a relatively high level of prolactin—a hormone known to promote parental care. **Where found:** shorelines, gravel beaches, drainage ditches, swamps and sewage lagoons; occasionally seen in cultivated fields; year-round resident of large streams. *Breeding:* throughout most of Northern California in summer.

Greater Yellowlegs

Tringa melanoleuca

Length: 13–15 in
Wingspan: 28 in

The greater yellowlegs and lesser yellowlegs (*T. flavipes*)
are medium-sized sandpipers with very similar plumages
and very yellow legs and feet. The species differ only subtly,
and a solitary greater yellowlegs is difficult to identify until it flushes and utters
its distinctive 3 peeps (the lesser yellowlegs peeps twice). As its name suggests, the
greater yellowlegs is the larger species and has a slightly upturned, longer bill.
Where found: any type of shallow wetland, whether freshwater, brackish or salt;
flooded agricultural fields.

Ring-billed Gull

Larus delawarensis

Length: 18–20 in
Wingspan: 4 ft

Few people can claim that they have never seen this
common and widespread gull. Highly tolerant of
humans, ring-billed gulls will eat almost anything
as they swarm parks, beaches, golf courses and fast-food parking lots looking for
food handouts and making pests of themselves. However, few species have
adjusted to human development as well as this gull, which is something to appreciate. • To differentiate between gulls, pay attention to the markings on their bills
and the color of their legs and eyes. **Where found:** a wide spectrum of open country foraging environments relatively close to water; common at garbage dumps.

California Gull

Larus californicus

Length: 18–20 in
Wingspan: 4–4½ ft

Despite its name, the California gull was a celebrated
hero in Utah when it ate hordes of crop-threaten-
ing grasshoppers in 1848 and 1855. There is a
monument in Salt Lake City honoring this
gull, which is now the Utah state bird. • The
world's largest colony of California gulls is at
Mono Lake. **Where found:** lakes, marshes, croplands, estuaries and open ocean to
miles offshore; cities and garbage dumps; most breed inland and winter on the
coast and into the western slopes of the mountains.

Western Gull

Larus occidentalis

Length: 24–26 in
Wingspan: 5 ft

This is "the" Pacific Coast seagull—one cannot overlook its conspicuous size and presence. It is a year-round resident on much of our coastline and is a colonial nester on coastal rocks with some vegetative cover. The western gull is not large in numbers, however, with fewer than 200 breeding colonies in total. There is concern that the effects of pesticides on reproduction, threats from oil spills and extensive hybridization with other gulls is compromising its population status. **Where found:** year-round coastal resident; offshore rocks, intertidal and shallow inshore zones, open ocean upwellings, coastal fields and coastal towns.

Caspian Tern

Sterna caspia

Length: 19–23 in
Wingspan: 4–4½ ft

The North American Caspian tern population has dramatically increased in the last half-century, mainly because of nesting habitat provided by human-made dredge-spoil islands and dikes. • Adults ferociously defend breeding colonies, aggressively attacking and dive-bombing potential predators, and are extremely sensitive to disturbance—birdwatchers are advised to keep their distance. • Believed to live an average of 12 years, the oldest wild Caspian tern lived more than 26 years! The caspian tern the largest tern in the world. **Where found:** beaches, mudflats, sandbars, lakes and flooded agricultural fields.

Forster's Tern

Sterna forsteri

Length: 14–16 in
Wingspan: 31 in

Forster's tern so closely resembles the common tern (*S. hirundo*) that the two often seem indistinguishable to the eyes of many observers. • Forster's tern has an exclusively North American breeding distribution, but it bears the name of a man who never visited this continent: German naturalist Johann Reinhold Forster (1729–98). Forster, who lived and worked in England, examined tern specimens sent from Hudson Bay, Canada, and recognized this bird as a distinct species. **Where found:** coastal areas, brackish wetlands and freshwater lakes, rivers and marshes; typically coastal in winter and inland in summer.

Marbled Murrelet

Brachyramphus marmoratus

Length: 9–10 in
Wingspan: 16 in

The marbled murrelet is one of the most unusual seabirds on the Pacific Coast. This secretive bird nests deep within the mossy heights of old-growth forests but returns to the ocean to feed. Each night for a month, adults bring their single, hungry nestling fish from the sea, sometimes flying 40 mi each way. Marbled murrelets' dependence on old-growth forests and coastal habitats often conflicts with human interests. **Where found:** along ocean shorelines and around harbor entrances; favors sandy bottoms opposite rocky shores. *Breeding:* dense, coniferous forests, particularly stands of old-growth coastal Douglas-fir.

Rock Pigeon

Columba livia

Length: 12–13 in
Wingspan: 28 in; male is usually larger

This pigeon is likely a descendant of a Eurasian bird that was first domesticated about 4500 BC. Both Caesar and Napoleon used rock pigeons as message couriers. European settlers introduced the rock pigeon to North America in the 17th century, and today, it is familiar to most anyone who has lived in a city. • No other "wild" bird varies as much in coloration, a result of semi-domestication and extensive inbreeding over time. **Where found:** urban areas, railway yards and agricultural areas; high cliffs often provide more natural habitat. **Also known as:** rock dove.

Band-tailed Pigeon

Columba fasciata

Length: 13–15 in
Wingspan: 26 in

Although similar in size, form and behavior to the familiar rock pigeon, band-tailed pigeons have a distinctive white crescent on the nape as well as a unique yellow bill and yellow legs. • Band-tailed pigeons range from nearly the southeastern tip of Alaska to northern Argentina. They feed by clinging clumsily to twigs that may scarcely support their weight while plucking at nuts and fruits. **Where found:** mixed conifer-hardwood forests and woodlands; canyons, foothills and lower mountains; backyards on the edge of stands of tall trees.

Mourning Dove

Zenaida macroura

Length: 11–13 in
Wingspan: 18 in

The mourning dove's soft cooing, which filters through broken woodlands and suburban parks, is often confused with the sound of a hooting owl. • This dove is one of the most abundant native birds in North America, with increased numbers and range since human development created more open habitats and food sources, such as waste grain and bird feeders. • Mourning doves lay only 2 eggs at a time, but up to 6 broods each year—more than any other native bird. **Where found:** open and riparian woodlands, forest edges, agricultural and suburban areas and parks.

Barn Owl

Tyto alba

Length: 12½–18 in
Wingspan: 3¾ ft

People and barn owls have a mutually beneficial relationship: we provide roosting and nesting structures such as barns and open hunting habitat such as croplands, and in return, these dedicated hunters keep rodent populations down. Their tolerance of and affiliation with human activity make them the most likely owls to encounter. **Where found:** roost and nest in cliffs, hollow trees, barns, mine shafts, caves, bridges and similar locations; require open areas such as agricultural fields, pastures, lawns, marshy meadows, open beaches or open streamside areas for hunting.

Great Horned Owl

Bubo virginianus

Length: 18–25 in
Wingspan: 3–5 ft

This highly adaptable and superbly camouflaged hunter has sharp hearing and powerful vision that allow it to hunt by night and day. It will swoop down from a perch onto almost any small creature that moves. • The leading edge of the flight feathers is fringed rather than smooth, which interrupts airflow over the wing and allows the owl to fly noiselessly. • The great horned owl has a poor sense of smell, which might explain why it is the only consistent predator of skunks. **Where found:** fragmented forests, fields, riparian woodlands, suburban parks and wooded edges of landfills.

Spotted Owl

Strix occidentalis

Length: 17–19 in
Wingspan: 3½ ft

The spotted owl unwittingly became the center of public attention in the Pacific Northwest when protecting this endangered species threatened to halt logging in coastal old-growth forests that this owl and many other species require to survive. The spotted owl has become a symbol for preserving this unique habitat and a reminder to balance the value of nature with our economic values. Spotted owl habitat is often dominated by Douglas-fir because the owl's main prey, flying squirrels, feed on a fungus that grows on fir trees. **Where found:** old-growth coniferous and mixed conifer-hardwood forest; wanderers or dispersing juveniles are occasionally well outside typical habitat.

White-throated Swift

Aeronautes saxatalis

Length: 6–7 in
Wingspan: 15 in

The white-throated swift is a true aeronaut (*Aeronautes* means "sky sailor")—only brief, cliff-clinging rest periods and annual nesting duties bring it to earth. This bird feeds, drinks, bathes and even mates while flying. As the name suggests, the swift is fast; it has been clocked at up to 200 mph—fast enough to avoid the talons of hungry falcons. **Where found:** Sierra Nevada and lower Coast ranges. *Breeding:* high cliffs, crags and dry escarpments in open country surrounded by coniferous forest; high desert fault blocks and river canyons; ranges widely in search of food. *In migration:* also at lower elevations.

Anna's Hummingbird

Calypte anna

Length: 3–4 in
Wingspan: 5–5½ in

Once restricted as a nesting species to the Pacific slope of northern Baja California and Southern California, Anna's hummingbird expanded its range northward along the coast after the 1930s, and today, we get to enjoy this beautiful hummer. • Hummingbirds are easily lured to our gardens with exotic, nectar-producing plants or hummingbird feeders. **Where found:** fairly common year-round resident west of the Sierra Nevada; warm, semi-open, lightly wooded country outside of the high mountains; retreats to lowlands and towns in winter.

Belted Kingfisher

Ceryle alcyon

Length: 11–14 in
Wingspan: 20–21 in

Perched on a bare branch over a productive pool, the "king of the fishers" plunges headfirst into the water, snatches up a fish or a frog, flips it into the air then swallows it headfirst. Nestlings are able to swallow small fish whole at only 5 days old. • In Greek mythology, Alcyon, the daughter of the wind god, grieved so deeply for her drowned husband that the gods transformed them both into kingfishers. **Where found:** rivers, large streams, lakes, marshes and beaver ponds, especially near exposed soil banks, gravel pits or bluffs.

Acorn Woodpecker

Melanerpes formicivorus

Length: 9 in
Wingspan: 15–17 in

The highly social acorn woodpecker lives in cohesive family groups of up to 16 birds, which commonly stay together year round to protect communal food stores (mainly acorns stored in hole-studded "granary trees") and nesting sites. During the breeding season, only 1 or 2 pairs will actually mate and produce eggs, which are laid in a single large nest cavity. Non-breeding members of the group help incubate the eggs and raise the young. **Where found:** oak forests, riparian woodlands and parks throughout most of wooded Northern California.

Red-breasted Sapsucker

Sphyrapicus rubber

Length: 8½ in
Wingspan: 16–17 in

The shy and inconspicuous nature of the red-breasted sapsucker contrasts with the bold, red-headed looks. • Sapsuckers drill rows of small holes in the trunks of trees and tall shrubs, later collecting oozing sap and trapped insects. They also eat the soft cambium layer growing beneath the bark. **Where found:** *Breeding:* moist, coniferous forests and broken mixed woodlands, often close to riparian areas. *In migration* and *winter:* a wide variety of lowland woodlands, parks, gardens and exotic tree plantations.

Nuttall's Woodpecker

Picoides nuttallii

Length: 7–7½ in
Wingspan: 13½ in

Probing in crevices and flaking off bark in search of wood-boring insects, insect eggs and ants, Nuttall's woodpecker hops acrobatically on the undersides of branches and deftly scales tree trunks. • Thomas Nuttall traveled across the country writing about natural history; his many contributions to ornithology include his *Manual of Ornithology of the United States and Canada*. **Where found:** permanent resident in foothill and valley bottoms; woodlands, particularly oak, throughout much of the interior and near the coast from Sonoma County southward.

Downy Woodpecker

Picoides pubescens

Length: 6–7 in
Wingspan: 12 in

A bird feeder well stocked with peanut butter and black-oil sunflower seeds may attract a pair of downy woodpeckers to your backyard. These approachable little birds are more tolerant of human activity than most other species, and they visit feeders more often than the larger, more aggressive hairy woodpeckers (*P. villosus*). • Downy woodpeckers have white outer tail feathers with several dark spots, whereas those of hairy woodpeckers are pure white. **Where found:** any wooded environment, especially deciduous and mixed forests and areas with tall, deciduous shrubs.

Northern Flicker

Colaptes auratus

Length: 12–13 in
Wingspan: 20 in

The northern flicker scours the ground and tree trunks in search of invertebrates, particularly ants that it squashes and preens itself with for the formic acid, which kills small parasites on its skin and feathers. • There are 2 races of northern flicker: the yellow-shafted flicker of eastern North America has yellow underwings and undertail coverts; the red-shafted flicker of the West has reddish underwings and undertail coverts. The red-shafted race is the widespread breeder in our area, but some yellow-shafts appear as migrants and winter residents. **Where found:** most broken or open forests, woodlands, forest edges, fields and meadows, riparian woodlands and suburban parks and gardens to an elevation of 10,000 ft; retreats from the highest elevations in winter.

Pileated Woodpecker

Dryocopus pileatus

Length: 16–17 in
Wingspan: 28–29 in

The pileated woodpecker, with its flaming red crest, chisel-like bill and commanding size, requires 100 acres of mature forest as a home territory. • A foraging pileated woodpecker leaves a large, rectangular cavity up to 12 in long at the base of a tree. • A pair of woodpeckers will spend up to 6 weeks excavating a large nest cavity in a dead or decaying tree. **Where found:** extensive tracts of old-growth or mature mixed and coniferous forests from near sea level to 7500 ft; also riparian woodlands or woodlots in suburban and agricultural areas.

Western Wood-Pewee

Contopus sordidulus

Length: 5–6 in
Wingspan: 10½ in

Aspiring birders will quickly come to recognize the burry, down-slurred call of the western wood-pewee as one of the most common summertime noises. • The nest is a model of concealment, looking like little more than a bump on a limb, but if it is discovered by predators, this flycatcher will aggressively defend it. • Overall numbers of western wood-pewees appear to be declining, potentially because of loss or alteration of habitat through clear-cutting or grazing. **Where found:** most semi-open forest habitats including cottonwood riparian, ponderosa pine and montane coniferous or mixed woodlands, orchards and residential woodlots.

Black Phoebe

Sayornis nigricans

Length: 6½–7 in
Wingspan: 10½–11 in

This phoebe is able to capture just about any insect that zips past its perch with delicate sallies from perch to ground. The black phoebe will sometimes catch prey on the water surface, perching on high rocks when tree limbs are unavailable, and may even catch small fish on occasion. **Where found:** year-round resident near water in semi-open habitats including riparian woodlands, steep-walled canyons, cities and farmlands with wet areas; typically from sea level to 4000 ft.

Ash-throated Flycatcher

Myiarchus cinerascens

Length: 7–8 in
Wingspan: 12 in

The hot, midday, summer air in the foothills of Northern California may often be filled with 3 dominant sounds: distant human activities, the droning of annual cicadas and the shrill, whistled calls of ash-throated flycatchers. These opportunistic, secondary cavity nesters will use a bluebird box, junked machinery or an unused mailbox if a tree cavity cannot be found. **Where found:** arid and semi-arid oak and coniferous woodlands at lower and middle elevations. *Breeding:* taller mixed chaparral, oak groves and woodlands; riparian corridors with large, old trees. *In migration:* wide variety of tree and shrub associations.

Western Kingbird

Tyrannus verticalis

Length: 8–9 in
Wingspan: 15½ in

Kingbirds are a group of flycatchers that perch on wires or fence posts in open habitats and fearlessly chase out larger birds from their breeding territories. • In tumbling aerial courtship displays, the male flies to heights of 65 ft above the ground, stalls, then tumbles and flips his way back to the earth. **Where found:** *Breeding:* irrigated valleys, open or riparian woodlands and woodland edges. *In migration* and *winter:* any fairly open habitat.

Loggerhead Shrike

Lanius ludovicianus

Length: 9 in
Wingspan: 12 in

These predatory songbirds perch atop trees and on wires to scan for small prey, which is caught in fast, direct flight or a swooping dive. Males display their hunting prowess by impaling prey on thorns or barbed wire. Many shrikes become traffic fatalities when they fly low across roads to prey on insects attracted to the warm pavement. • The loggerhead shrike is an endangered species in North America. **Where found:** open country adjacent to dense brush; savannah and oak woodlands, ranches with grazed pastures and marginal and abandoned farmlands with scattered hawthorn shrubs, fence posts, barbed wire and nearby wetlands.

Hutton's Vireo

Vireo huttoni

Length: 4–5 in
Wingspan: 8 in

In early spring, male Hutton's vireos sing continuously throughout the day, waging vocal battles in an attempt to defend their nesting territories. Their song is an oscillating *zuWEEM, zuWEEM, zuWEEM.* They can be attracted with persistent "pishing" and are quite numerous; thus the odds of seeing one are higher than beginner birders might expect. **Where found:** year-round resident in Northern California's oak and pine-oak woodlands; partial to live oak and tanoak.

Steller's Jay

Cyanocitta stelleri

Length: 11–12 in
Wingspan: 19 in

With a dark crest and velvet blue feathers, the stunning Steller's jay is a resident jewel in Northern California's forests. Generally noisy and pugnacious, this bird suddenly becomes silent and cleverly elusive when nesting. • Bold Steller's jays will not hesitate to steal food scraps from inattentive picnickers and scatter smaller birds at feeders. Their ability to adapt, learn and even take advantage of situations shows the intelligence of corvids. **Where found:** widespread resident throughout forested Northern California; irregular visitor to the lowlands, most often in fall and winter.

Western Scrub-Jay

Aphelocoma californica

Length: 11½ in
Wingspan: 16 in

This intelligent corvid harvests fallen acorns and stores them in holes that it has dug into the ground with its strong bill; it uses a rock or concrete slab as a type of anvil to crack them open. Any acorns the western scrub-jay does not eat have been effectively planted, and many germinate and regenerate the oak stands. **Where found:** common year-round resident of chaparral and dry, brushy, open areas of oak and pinyon-juniper woodlands, mixed oak-conifer forests and riparian woodlands; also found in suburban parks and gardens.

Black-billed Magpie

Pica hudsonia

Length: 18 in
Wingspan: 25 in

Truly among North America's most beautiful birds, black-billed magpies are also exceptional architects, building elaborate, domed, stick and twig nests held together with mud. They are famed interior designers as well, picking up any shiny objects they can carry to decorate their nests with. These prized homes have a high resale value, remaining in trees for years and being used by other birds. • Albino magpies occasionally occur, with white bellies and light gray, instead of black, body feathers. **Where found:** open forests, agricultural areas, riparian thickets, townsites and campgrounds.

American Crow

Corvus brachyrhynchos

Length: 17–21 in
Wingspan: 36 in

The noise that most often emanates from these treetop squawkers seems unrepresentative of their intelligence. Crows will often drop walnuts or clams from great heights onto a hard surface to crack the shells. These wary, clever birds are also impressive mimics, able to whine like a dog and laugh or cry like a human. • Crows are family oriented, and the young from the previous year may help their parents raise the nestlings. **Where found:** urban areas, agricultural fields and other open areas with scattered woodlands.

Common Raven

Corvus corax

Length: 21–23 in
Wingspan: 4 ft

The common raven soars with a wingspan comparable to that of hawk, traveling along coastlines, over deserts, along mountain ridges and even over the arctic tundra. Few birds occupy such a large natural range. • From producing complex vocalizations to playfully sliding down snowbanks, this raucous bird exhibits behaviors that many people once thought of as exclusively human. Glorified in Native American culture, the raven seems to demonstrate an apparent enjoyment of life. **Where found:** coniferous and mixed forests and woodlands; townsites, campgrounds and landfills.

Horned Lark

Eremophila alpestris

Length: 7 in
Wingspan: 12 in

One way to distinguish a sparrow from a horned lark is by its method of locomotion: horned larks walk, but sparrows hop. • This bird's dark tail contrasts with its light brown body and belly, and it has 2 unique black "horns." Look for this feature to spot the horned lark in its open-country habitat. • In spring, the male performs an impressive, high-speed, plummeting courtship dive. **Where found:** treeless, open country; barren-ground and short-grass habitats from sea level to over 12,000 ft.

Cliff Swallow

Petrochelidon pyrrhonota

Length: 5½ in
Wingspan: 13½ in

Cliff swallows nest on various human-made structures such as bridges, culverts and eaves. Entire colonies under bridges can be wiped out during floods. Master mud masons, cliff swallows roll mud into balls with their bills and press the pellets together to form their characteristic gourd-shaped nests. **Where found:** *Breeding:* cliffs, caves, rimrocks, ocean bluffs, bridges, buildings, tunnels, dams, viaducts and mine shafts from sea level to 9000 ft. *In migration:* open lowland areas including meadows, farmlands, golf courses, beaches, rivers and marshes.

Barn Swallow

Hirundo rustica

Length: 7 in
Wingspan: 15 in

The messy young and aggressive parents unfortunately often motivate people to remove barn swallow nests just as nesting season is beginning, but this bird's close association with humans allows us to observe the normally secretive nesting time for birds. • The barn swallow is a natural pest controller, feeding on insects that are often harmful to crops and livestock and annoying to humans. **Where found:** *Breeding:* rural and suburban buildings from sea level to 5000 ft; sea cliffs and caves. *In migration:* varied open lowland areas; meadows, farmlands, parks, freshwater lakes, rivers, marshes, estuaries and beaches.

Chestnut-backed Chickadee

Poecile rufescens

Length: 5½ in
Wingspan: 7½ in

One chestnut-backed chickadee could fit in the palm of your hand, but these energetic little birds would hardly sit still long enough. They prefer to flit through the forest and scour for insects or descend on bird feeders in merry mobs. To view these friendly birds up close, mount a platform feeder on your window ledge. • Mountain chickadees (*P. gambeli*) and black-capped chickadees (*P. atricapillus*) are also found in Northern California. **Where found:** coniferous, hardwood and mixed forests; various native and exotic trees in residential areas; backyard feeders.

Oak Titmouse

Baeolophus inornatus

Length: 5–5½ in
Wingspan: 7½ in

The nasal *tsick-a-dee-dee* call of the oak titmouse is a characteristic sound of the sprawling oak woodlands of interior Northern California west of the Sierra-Cascades. • The oak titmouse nests in natural cavities, rotted stumps and occasionally in abandoned woodpecker nests. The female will fill the cavity with vegetation, feathers and hair and incubate her 6–8 eggs for about 2 weeks. The parents mate for life, and both feed the young. **Where found:** year round in mixed oak and riparian woodlands.

Bushtit

Psaltriparus minimus

Length: 4–4½ in
Wingspan: 6 in

Bushtits catch your eye as they endlessly bounce from one shrubby perch to another and catch you ear with charming, bell-like, tinkling calls. Hyperactive in everything they do, these tiny, fluffy, gregarious birds are constantly on the move, either fastidiously building a nest or roaming about in post-breeding bands of up to 40 members. When nest building, they neurotically test every fiber to ensure its suitability. • Bushtits will desert both nest and mate if intruded upon. **Where found:** year-round western residents of juniper and oak forests, riparian brushlands, chaparral and large, residential gardens.

White-breasted Nuthatch

Sitta carolinensis

Length: 5½–6 in
Wingspan: 11 in

Its upside-down antics and noisy, nasal call make the white-breasted nuthatch a favorite among novice birders. Whether you spot this black-capped bullet spiraling headfirst down a tree or clinging to the underside of a branch in search of invertebrates, its odd behavior deserves a second glance. • Nuthatches are presumably named for their habit of wedging seeds and nuts into crevices and hacking them open with their bills. **Where found:** year-round resident of pine forests, oak woodlands, backyards and along the Sacramento River.

Bewick's Wren

Thryomanes bewickii

Length: 5–5½ in
Wingspan: 7 in

This charming wren scans its surroundings with endless curiosity and exuberant animations as its long, narrow tail flits and waves from side to side. It is always on the lookout for insects to prey upon or intruders to angrily scold. **Where found:** year-round resident at lower and middle elevations; chaparral, riparian thickets, parks, gardens and brush piles; dense vines and shrubby tangles bordering woodlands and shrublands within pinyon-juniper and oak woodlands.

Ruby-crowned Kinglet

Regulus calendula

Length: 4 in
Wingspan: 7½ in

This kinglet's familiar voice echoes through our boreal forest in spring and summer. Not only does the male ruby-crowned kinglet possess a loud, complex, warbling song to bring him some attention, but he also wears a nifty red "mohawk" to help attract a mate and defend his territory in spring. Unfortunately, his distinctive crown is only visible in breeding season, leaving him with just his dull, olive green plumage for the rest of the year. **Where found:** *Breeding:* subalpine coniferous forests at 4000–10,000 ft. *In migration* and *winter:* practically all trees and shrubbery.

Western Bluebird

Sialia mexicana

Length: 7 in
Wingspan: 13½ in

Like the feathers of all bluebirds, western bluebird feathers
are not actually pigmented blue. The color is a result of the
feathers' microscopic structure, which produces various hues
of blue by iridescence or by the Tyndall effect, which is the same
process that causes the sky to be blue. • Western bluebirds usually
succeed in raising 2 broods, producing the second clutch of eggs as soon as the
first brood leaves the nest. **Where found:** *Breeding:* broken oak and oak-conifer
woodlands, oak savannahs, riparian woodlands and open pine forests; near sea
level to 7000 ft. *In migration* and *winter:* lowland valleys, agricultural lands interspersed with woodlands and tree groves; northwest coastal lowlands.

Hermit Thrush

Catharus guttatus

Length: 7 in
Wingspan: 11½ in

The hermit thrush's haunting, flute-like song may be one
of the most beautiful natural melodies, and it is almost
always preceded with a single questioning note. • This
thrush feeds mainly on insects, worms and snails during summer, but it adds
a wide variety of fruit to its winter diet. **Where found:** *Breeding:* well-shaded coniferous
and high evergreen-oak forests; often on ridges on upper hillsides; montane riparian
areas; near sea level to 10,000 ft; open pine and aspen forests at 7000–10,000 ft east of
the Sierra-Cascades. *In migration* and *winter:* varied dense, low vegetation.

American Robin

Turdus migratorius

Length: 10 in
Wingspan: 17 in

The American robin is a familiar
and common sight on lawns as it
searches for worms. In winter, its
diet switches to fruit, which can attract flocks to fruit trees to feed. • American
robins build cup-shaped nests of grass, moss and mud. The female incubates
4 light blue eggs and raises up to 3 broods per year. The male cares for the fledg-
lings from the first brood while the female incubates the second clutch of eggs.
Where found: riparian woodlands, forests with open meadows and forest edges.

Wrentit

Chamaea fasciata

Length: 6–6½ in
Wingspan: 7 in

Unlike most songbirds, wrentits do not migrate, and they mate for life. They are secretive birds, preferring to remain concealed within dense tangles of brush and scrub and rarely cross open areas where predators could interrupt their feeble flights without warning. A pair of wrentits may spend an entire lifetime together in an area no larger than a few acres. **Where found:** hilly brushlands, lowland and montane chaparral, coastal sage scrub, northern coastal scrub and shrubby tangles along the edges of streams and suburban gardens; readily colonize regenerating logged sites.

European Starling

Sturnus vulgaris

Length: 8½ in
Wingspan: 16 in

The European starling spread across North America after being released in New York City's Central Park in 1890 and 1891. Starlings were brought to New York as part of the local Shakespeare society's plan to introduce all the birds mentioned in their favorite author's writings. • This highly adaptable bird not only takes over the nest sites of native cavity nesters, such as wood-peckers, but it also mimics the sounds of killdeers, red-tailed hawks, soras and meadowlarks. **Where found:** *Breeding:* cities, towns, residential areas, farmyards and woodland fringes and clearings. *Winter:* near feedlots and pastures.

Cedar Waxwing

Bombycilla cedrorum

Length: 7 in
Wingspan: 12 in

With its black mask and slick hairdo, the cedar waxwing has a heroic look. To court a mate, the gentlemanly male hops toward a female and offers her a berry. The female accepts the berry and hops away, then stops and hops back toward the male to offer him the berry in return. **Where found:** *Breeding:* hardwood and mixed forests, woodland edges, fruit orchards, young pine plantations and riparian hard-woods among conifers. *In migration* and *winter:* open woodlands and brush, residential areas and any habitat with berries nearby; often near water.

Orange-crowned Warbler

Vermivora celata

Length: 5 in
Wingspan: 7 in

The nondescript orange-crowned warbler causes identification problems for many birders. Its drab, olive yellow appearance and lack of field marks make it frustratingly similar to females of other warbler species, and the male's orange crown patch is seldom visible. • This small warbler is usually seen gleaning insects from the leaves and buds of low shrubs and routinely feeds on sap or insects attracted to the sap wells drilled by other birds. **Where found:** any wooded habitat; areas with tall shrubs.

Yellow-rumped Warbler

Dendroica coronata

Length: 5½ in
Wingspan: 9–9½ in

Yellow-rumped warblers are the most abundant and widespread wood-warblers in North America. Trees laden with fruit attract these birds in winter. • This species comes in 2 forms: the yellow-throated "Audubon's warbler" of the West, and the white-throated "myrtle warbler," which breeds in the North and east of the Rockies. Myrtle warblers do not breed in Northern California, but they are commonly seen in winter and during migration along the Pacific Coast. **Where found:** hardwood and mixed thickets and woodlands along the coast; interior valleys.

Common Yellowthroat

Geothlypis trichas

Length: 5 in
Wingspan: 7 in

The bumblebee colors of the male common yellowthroat's black mask and yellow throat identify this skulking wetland resident. The male sings his *witchety* song from strategically chosen cattail perches that he visits in rotation, fiercely guarding his territory against the intrusion of other males. • Many wetland species have been displaced in Northern California, especially in the Central Valley, because of urban and agricultural development. **Where found:** cattail marshes, sedge wetlands, riparian areas, beaver ponds and wet, overgrown meadows; sometimes dry fields.

Western Tanager

Piranga ludoviciana

Length: 7 in
Wingspan: 11–11½ in

The western tanager brings with it the colors of a tropical visitor on its summer vacation in our area. This bird raises a new generation of young and takes advantage of the seasonal explosion of food in our forests before heading back to its exotic wintering grounds in Mexico and Central America. • The male western tanager spends long periods of time singing from the same perch, sounding similar to a robin with a sore throat. **Where found:** mature coniferous and mixed forests, especially ponderosa pine. *In migration:* fruit-bearing trees and shrubs in riparian woodlands.

California Towhee

Pipilo crissalis

Length: 8½–10 in
Wingspan: 12 in

California towhees are highly territorial and will proclaim their territory by singing out with a sharp, metallic *chink*. They are so territorial that male towhees have been observed attacking their own reflections in low-mounted windows. Yet, they are very accepting of their human neighbors and are commonly seen foraging under picnic tables, on patios or at the feet of admiring birders. **Where found:** broken chaparral and shrubby tangles, thickets and hedgerows near streams; gardens, parks, farmyards and woodlands.

Savannah Sparrow

Passerculus sandwichensis

Length: 5–6½ in
Wingspan: 8½–9 in

Like most sparrows, the savannah sparrow generally prefers to stay out of sight, although small flocks and individuals are sometimes seen darting across roads, fields or beaches. It is not apt to fly even if threatened, preferring to run swiftly and inconspicuously through tall grasses as an escape tactic. **Where found:** *Breeding:* coastal grasslands, estuary meadows, salt marshes, grassy interior valleys and borders of mountain streams, agricultural fields and alkaline lakeshores. *Winter:* fields, grasslands and coastline.

Fox Sparrow

Passerella iliaca

Length: 6½–7½ in
Wingspan: 10½ in

Fox sparrows spend most of their time on the ground, scratching away leaf litter and duff to expose seeds and insects. • The approximately 15 sub-species of fox sparrow in California exhibit an array of color variations; *P. i. stephensi* and other subspecies that nest in the Sierra Nevada (but winter elsewhere) have a gray head and back contrasting with rusty wings, rump and tail. **Where found:** *Breeding:* mountain slopes at 3000–9600 ft; montane chaparral and riparian areas. *In migration* and *winter:* brushy lowland thickets, parks, gardens and suburban backyards.

Song Sparrow

Melospiza melodia

Length: 6–7 in
Wingspan: 8 in

Although its plumage is unremarkable, the well-named song sparrow is among the great singers of the bird world. When a male song sparrow is only a few months old, he has already created a courtship tune of his own, having learned the basics of melody and rhythm from his father and rival males. A well-stocked backyard feeder may be a fair trade for a sweet song in the dead of winter. **Where found:** hardwood brush in forests and open country; near water or in lush vegetation in chaparral, riparian willows, marshy habitats and residential areas.

White-crowned Sparrow

Zonotrichia leucophrys

Length: 5½–7 in
Wingspan: 9½ in

In winter, large, bold and smartly patterned white-crowned sparrows brighten brushy hedgerows, overgrown fields and riparian areas. During cold weather, these sparrows may visit bird feeders stocked with cracked corn. • Several different races of white-crowned sparrow occur in North America, all with similar plumage but different song dialects. Research into this sparrow has given science tremendous insight into bird physiology, homing behavior and the geographic variability of song dialects. **Where found:** areas with a mix of shrub or tree cover and more open ground; in mixed flocks in residential areas, parks, gardens and unplowed croplands.

Dark-eyed Junco

Junco hyemalis

Length: 6–7 in
Wingspan: 9 in

Juncos usually congregate in backyards with bird feeders and sheltering conifers—with such amenities at their disposal, more and more juncos are appearing in urban areas. These birds spend most of their time on the ground, snatching up seeds underneath bird feeders, and they are readily flushed from wooded trails. • There are 5 closely related dark-eyed junco subspecies in North America that share similar habits but differ in coloration and range. **Where found:** shrubby woodland borders and backyard feeders.

Black-headed Grosbeak

Pheucticus melanocephalus

Length: 7–8½ in
Wingspan: 12½ in

Black-headed grosbeaks will quickly make your acquaintance on almost any spring or summer hike in the woods. These birds are marvelous singers, advertising breeding territories with extended bouts of complex, accented caroling. Males sing from slightly sheltered perches near the top of a tree, while females forage and conduct nesting chores within the cover of interior foliage. **Where found:** hardwood and mixed forests; bottomland willows and cottonwoods, riparian and lakeshore woodlands, rich oak woodlands and high-elevation aspen groves.

Red-winged Blackbird

Agelaius phoeniceus

Length: 7½–9 in
Wingspan: 13 in

The male red-winged blackbird wears his bright red shoulders like armor—together with his short, raspy song, they are key in defending his territory from rivals. • Nearly every cattail marsh worthy of note in our region hosts red-winged blackbirds and resonates with that proud and distinctive song. The female's cryptic coloration allows her to sit inconspicuously on her nest, blending in perfectly among the cattails or shoreline bushes. **Where found:** cattail marshes, wet meadows and ditches, croplands and shoreline shrubs.

Western Meadowlark

Sturnella neglecta

Length: 9–9½ in
Wingspan: 14½ in

In the early 19th century, members of the Lewis and Clark expedition overlooked the western meadowlark, mistaking it for the very similar-looking eastern meadowlark, hence the scientific name *neglecta*. • A breeding pair bond is established with an elaborate courtship dance; the male and female face each other, raise their bills high in the air and perform a grassland ballet. • Western meadowlarks have benefited from land management that protects grasslands from over-grazing or agriculture. **Where found:** grassy meadows, native prairie and pastures; also in some croplands, weedy fields and grassy roadsides.

Brewer's Blackbird

Euphagus cyanocephalus

Length: 8–10 in
Wingspan: 15–15½ in

Urban and agricultural development has been very beneficial to Brewer's blackbird. Agriculture and ranching provide ample forage opportunities, and landscaped trees and tall shrubs offer sheltered nesting sites. This bird has also found a niche opportunistically feeding on road-killed insects. **Where found:** wet meadows, grasslands, shores, roadsides, landfills, golf courses, urban and suburban parks and gardens, ranches, farmyards, pastures and freshwater marshes from sea level to nearly 9000 ft.

Brown-headed Cowbird

Molothrus ater

Length: 6–8 in
Wingspan: 12 in

These nomads historically followed bison herds across the Great Plains (they now follow cattle), so they never stayed in one area long enough to build and tend a nest. Instead, brown-headed cowbirds lay their eggs in the nests of other birds and have become the most successful brood parasites in North America. **Where found:** agricultural and residential areas, fields, woodland edges, utility cutlines, roadsides, fencelines, landfills, campgrounds and areas near cattle.

House Finch

Carpodacus mexicanus

Length: 5–6 in
Wingspan: 9½ in

Formerly restricted to the arid Southwest and Mexico, the house finch is now commonly found throughout the continental U.S. and has even been introduced to Hawaii. Only the resourceful house finch has been aggressive and stubborn enough to successfully outcompete the house sparrow. • The male house finch's plumage varies in color from light yellow to bright red, but females will choose to breed with the reddest males. **Where found:** disturbed areas, including farms, ranches and towns; open fields and woodlands. *Winter:* backyard feeders.

Pine Siskin

Carduelis pinus

Length: 4½–5½ in
Wingspan: 9 in

Pine siskins are unpredictable, social birds that may be abundant for a time, then suddenly disappear. Because their favored habitats are widely scattered, flocks are constantly on the move, searching forests for the most lucrative seed crops. • These drab, sparrow-like birds are easy to overlook at first, but once you recognize their characteristic rising *zzzreeeee* calls and boisterous chatter, you will encounter them with surprising frequency. **Where found:** coniferous forests, though not pines as its name suggests; backyard finch feeders of black niger seed.

Lesser Goldfinch

Carduelis psaltria

Length: 4–4½ in
Wingspan: 8 in

The preference of the lesser goldfinch for dry, weedy expanses and proximity to fresh water of any description animates the often dramatic contrast between a Northern Californian watercourse and its arid surroundings. The distinctive song that indicates its presence is a breezy, closely knit exclamation involving call-notes, chattering and snatches of songs and calls from other bird species. **Where found:** various semi-open habitats that provide nest cover, seeds, insects and water; oak woodlands, chaparral and the edges of suburban and rural areas.

American Goldfinch

Carduelis tristis

Length: 4½–5 in
Wingspan: 9 in

Like vibrant rays of sunshine, American goldfinches cheerily flutter over weedy fields, gardens and along roadsides, perching on late-summer thistle heads or poking through dandelion patches in search of seeds. It is hard to miss their jubilant *po-ta-to-chip* call and distinctive, undulating flight style. • Because these acrobatic birds regularly feed while hanging upside down, finch feeders are designed with the seed openings below the perches. **Where found:** weedy fields, woodland edges, meadows, riparian areas, parks and gardens. **Also known as:** willow goldfinch.

House Sparrow

Passer domesticus

Length: 5½–6½ in
Wingspan: 9½ in

This abundant and conspicuous bird was introduced to North America in the 1850s as part of a plan to control the insects that were damaging grain and cereal crops. As it turns out, these birds are largely vegetarian! • The house sparrow will usurp territory and nests of other native birds, such as bluebirds, cliff swallows or purple martins, and has a high reproductive output of 4 clutches per year, with up to 8 young per clutch. **Where found:** townsites, urban and suburban areas, farmyards and agricultural areas, railway yards and other developed areas.

AMPHIBIANS & REPTILES

Amphibians and reptiles are commonly referred to as cold-blooded, but this is misleading. Although these animals lack the ability to generate internal body heat, they are not necessarily cold-blooded. They are ectothermic or poikilothermic, meaning that the temperature of the surrounding environment governs their body temperature. The animal will obtain heat from sunlight, warm rocks and logs, and warmed earth. Reptiles and amphibians hibernate in winter in cold areas, and some reptiles estivate in summer in hot regions. Both amphibians and reptiles molt as they grow to larger body sizes.

Amphibians (salamanders, frogs and toads) are smooth-skinned and most live in moist habitats. They typically lay shell-less eggs in jelly-like masses in water. These eggs hatch into gilled larvae (e.g., tadpoles), which then metamorphose into adults with lungs and legs. Amphibians can regenerate their skin and often even entire limbs. Male and female amphibians often differ in size and color, and males may have other diagnostics when sexually mature, such as the vocal sacs in many frogs and toads.

Reptiles are fully terrestrial vertebrates with scaly skin. In this guide, the representatives are skinks, turtles and snakes. Most lay eggs buried in loose soil, but some snakes and lizards give birth to live young. Reptiles do not have a larval stage.

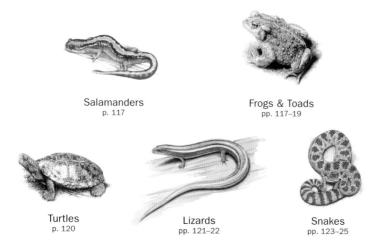

Salamanders
p. 117

Frogs & Toads
pp. 117–19

Turtles
p. 120

Lizards
pp. 121–22

Snakes
pp. 123–25

California Newt

Taricha torosa

Length: 5–8 in

The California newt lives a dual lifestyle as a terrestrial, nonbreeding eft before becoming an aquatic newt. As a terrestrial eft in late summer and fall, it hides under logs and in rock crevices; then at the first rains of winter, it migrates to the water and, upon entering, transforms into an aquatic newt and breeds. • It announces its toxicity to predators by showing off its bright orange underbelly, which it displays by arching its back, raising its head and pointing its tail and legs upward. **Where found:** moist forests from sea level to above 6000 ft in the Coast ranges and the western slopes of the Sierra Nevada.

California Tiger Salamander

Ambystoma californiense

Length: 6–8½ in

The increasingly rare California tiger salamander has been extirpated from more than half of its original range, and its current range is fragmented by agricultural development. It easily hybridizes with the non-native tiger salamander (*A. tigrinum*). • This fossorial species spends most of its time underground, emerging during the fall rains in mass migrations to breeding ponds. **Where found:** grasslands, oak savannahs, edges of mixed woodlands and low-elevation coniferous forests; endemic to California from Sonoma County south, with isolated populations in the Sacramento Valley.

Long-toed Salamander

Ambystoma macrodactylum

Length: 3–5 in

These striking, secretive creatures often hide under rocks or decomposing logs. They are active primarily at night, but they are more easily seen in the rainy months of April and May, when they migrate to their breeding sites in silt-free ponds and lakes. Eggs laid singly or in clumps on rocks or vegetation take about 3 weeks to hatch. • Long-toed salamanders feed on invertebrates. **Where found:** arid, low-elevation sagebrush to valley wetlands to subalpine forests; the only salamander to exist on both sides of the Cascade Mountains.

Great Basin Spadefoot

Spea intermontana

Length: 1½–2½ in

Named for the dark, wedge-shaped "spade" found near the heel of their hind feet, spadefoot toads burrow underground during the day and resurface at night to hunt for insects. A small hump between their eyes, called a boss, protects their heads when pushing their way through the soil to the surface. • These relatively smooth-skinned amphibians are not true toads because they lack parotid glands and warts; instead, they have small, lumpy, black and red tubercles on olive-green to grayish-green skin. **Where found:** arid regions east of the Sierra-Cascade ranges.

Western Toad

Bufo boreas

Length: 2–5 in

Touching a toad will not give you warts, but the western toad does have a way of discouraging unwanted affection. When handled, it secretes a toxin from large parotid glands behind its eyes that acts to irritate the mouth of potential predators. • This large, gray, green or brown toad is a voracious predator of insects and other tasty invertebrates such as worms and slugs. **Where found:** near springs, streams, meadows and woodlands throughout western California.

Coastal Tailed Frog

Ascaphus truei

Length: 1–2 in

Frigid mountain streams do not deter these tough little frogs. They lay their eggs on the downstream side of large rocks in fast-flowing streams to prevent them from being swept away in the current, and the tadpoles fastidiously cling to rocks with their suction cup–like mouths. • The adults vary in color from green to gray, brown or reddish brown. The "tail" is actually the male copulatory organ; these frogs are one of the very few species with internal fertilization. **Where found:** cold, fast-flowing mountain streams.

Bullfrog

Rana catesbeiana

Length: up to 8 in

Bullfrogs are not native to California but were introduced in the early 1900s. They are very large and live an average of 7–9 years, with records of captive individuals living 16 years.
• Bullfrogs are predatory, eating anything they can swallow, including certain snakes and fish, and are incredibly prolific, making them a significant threat to native frog populations. **Where found:** warm, still, shallow, vegetated waters of lakes, ponds, rivers and bogs.

Red-legged Frog

Rana aurora

Length: 2–5½ in

Once hunted for its prized legs for culinary purposes, this frog is now heavily preyed upon by bullfrogs. Habitat loss and water pollution are the red-legged frog's greatest threats. Sightings of this threatened native frog should be reported to the U.S. Fish and Wildlife Service. • The frog caught in a swamp near Angels Camp in Mark Twain's "The Notorious Jumping Frog of Calaveras County" was probably a red-legged frog. **Where found:** deep, still or slow-moving ponds or intermittent streams with emergent riparian vegetation; west of the Sierra-Cascade ranges.

Pacific Treefrog

Hyla regilla

Length: 1–2 in

Pacific treefrogs have adhesive toe pads that enable them to climb vertical surfaces and cling to the tiniest branch. The frogs can also change color within a few minutes, allowing them to blend into their immediate habitat. Colors include green, brown, gray, tan, reddish and black; dark spots are often present. • Despite their name, these frogs are often terrestrial, choosing moist, grassy habitats. **Where found:** low-elevation shrubby areas close to water; riparian areas. **Also known as:** *Pseudacris regilla*.

Western Pond Turtle

Clemmys marmorata

Length: 4–9 in

Unless they see you first and quickly disappear into the water, western pond turtles are typically seen either singly or in groups, basking in the sun on a rock or log in a pond. • Pond turtles feed mainly on crayfish, insects, amphibian eggs and larvae and aquatic plants. Raccoons, large fish and bullfrogs prey on pond turtle eggs and juveniles, but once the turtles mature, predation rates drop significantly. They can live over 50 years in the wild. **Where found:** mud-bottomed ponds, lakes, sloughs, marshes and slow-moving rivers in valleys; scattered locations throughout Northern California. **Also known as:** mud turtle.

Leatherback Sea Turtle

Dermochelys coriacea

Length: up to 9 ft

Leatherbacks show up sporadically along the California coast, especially when there is an abundance of jellyfish, their favored prey. In July 2000, a bloom of jellyfish in Monterey Bay attracted a number of leatherbacks, and in fall of 2006, several individuals were seen at Point Reyes, which is farther north than their typical range. Leatherbacks do not nest here, but on tropical beaches of South America. Sightings are mainly from whale-watching or pelagic bird-watching boats. • Leatherbacks can exceed 1 ton in wieght. **Where found:** oceans around the world; off the coast of California at the extreme north of their range.

Southern Alligator Lizard

Elgaria multicarinata

Length: 12 in

Think twice before picking up a southern alligator lizard because it is notorious for biting and, perhaps even worse, defecating foul-smelling feces. • This small lizard preys upon pretty much anything smaller than itself, which includes insects and spiders, scorpions, snails and slugs, worms, smaller lizards, baby mice and birds and bird eggs. **Where found:** oak woodlands and savannahs of the western foothills of the Cascade Mountains; pine and mixed oak-pine and brushy chaparral of the Klamath Mountains.

Sagebrush Lizard

Sceloporus graciosus

Length: 1½–5½ in

Sagebrush lizards hunt insects, spiders, mites and ticks on the ground or in shrubs. They bask on sun-warmed rocks or hide in shady bushes to maintain their body temperature; studies report lizards allowing themselves to overheat in hot sun to induce a form of fever to break bacterial infections. • Males have blue belly patches and mottling on the throat; the pink sides and neck become brighter on females during breeding season. Sagebrush lizards do not have the large, pointed dorsal scales typical of *Sceloporus* species. **Where found:** dry areas with sagebrush; both sides of the Cascade Mountains and in the chaparral areas of the Klamath Mountains.

Western Fence Lizard

Sceloporus occidentalis

Length: 7 in

Bright blue patches on the sides of the abdomen and under the throat (though on the female, this coloring can be faded or lacking) as well as prickly looking scales on the back are diagnostic of the western fence lizard. The males flaunt their bright blue bellies during breeding season in much the same way that many gloriously plumed male birds do to impress females and challenge rival males, with which they will aggressively fight. **Where found:** open, sunny areas with logs, fence posts or rocks to bask on; valleys, mountains, oak woodlands and coastal areas west of the Sierra-Cascades. **Also known as:** blue-bellied lizard.

Western Whiptail

Cnemidophorus tigris

Length: 13 in

Mostly tail, with a body length of only 2½–4½ in, the western whiptail adds on another significant length by sticking out its impressively long forked tongue. • For food, it digs for buried insects, spiders, scorpions and occasionally other lizards. • A juvenile western whiptail has a pale blue to bluish-gray tail, which often leads to it being mistaken for a western skink. **Where found:** arid flats and hillsides of sagebrush or other shrubby areas; oak and chaparral regions; northeastern California, specifically Honey Lake Basin and Surprise Valley; the Sacramento River drainage area of Northern California.

Western Skink

Eumeces skiltonianus

Length: 7½ in

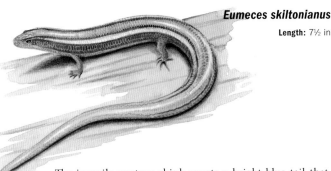

The juvenile western skink sports a bright blue tail that, when grabbed by predators, easily breaks off and continues to writhe while the skink makes its escape; it will soon grow a new tail. An adult's tail fades to become reddish orange during breeding season. • Skinks feed on insects and spiders. **Where found:** among leaf litter and underneath bark and rocks; burrows in grasslands, woodlands, pine forests, sagebrush and chaparral; rocky areas near streams with plenty of vegetation; throughout the northern Sierra Nevada and foothills and in the Coast Mountain ranges from sea level to about 8300 ft; not present in the central valleys.

Yellow-bellied Racer

Coluber constrictor

Length: 2–7 ft

The racer relies on speed to catch prey and escape danger. On the ground, it moves with its head held high for a better view of the terrain; it will also climb shrubs to find birds and insects. • Certain individuals have a bluish cast to the body. **Where found:** open forests, wooded hills, grassy ditches and riparian areas; oak, chaparral and grassy savannah regions west of the Sierra-Cascades; open juniper and pine forests, rocky canyons and sagebrush flats east of the mountains.

Western Rattlesnake

Crotalus viridis

Length: average 16–36 in; up to 4 ft and rarely to 5 ft

The subspecies of western rattlesnake that lives in Northern California is the Northern Pacific rattlesnake (*C. v. oreganus*). • Generally unappreciated by humans, the rattlesnake plays an important ecological role, preying upon rodents and other small mammals. It is the only venomous reptile native to the Northwest. • A rattlesnake bite is painful but rarely lethal to an adult unless left untreated for several hours. • Rattlesnakes are born live with a "button" rattle, to which an additional segment is added with each molt. **Where found:** dry areas east of the Sierra-Cascade ranges and the interior valleys of Northern California.

Common Gartersnake

Thamnophis sirtalis

Length: 20–51 in

Swift on land and in water, the common garter snake is an efficient hunter of amphibians, fish, small mammals, slugs and leeches. Some populations have shown resistance to the toxins produced by the western toad and the California newt and will prey upon them as well. • A single female can give birth to a litter of 3–83 young, but typically no more than 18. **Where found:** aquatic habitats throughout Northern California from sea level to just over 7000 ft.

Gophersnake

Pituophis catenifer

Length: 2½–6 ft

This large, beautiful constrictor is often mistaken for a rattlesnake because of its similar coloration, patterning and aggressive defensive strategy. When threatened, it hisses and vibrates its tail against vegetation, often producing a rattling sound. • The gophersnake frequently overwinters in communal dens with other snakes, including rattlesnakes, garter snakes and racers. **Where found:** open, dry, oak savannahs, brushy chaparral, meadows and sparse, sunny areas in coniferous forests; common in the dry areas of the Klamath Mountains. **Also known as:** bullsnake.

Common Kingsnake

Lampropeltis getula

Length: 24–45 in

The non-venomous common kingsnake is distinctly black-and-white-striped, though some of these snakes in the Sacramento River drainage are dark brown with creamy yellow stripes. • The kingsnake feeds on other reptiles, including rattlesnakes, to whose venom it is immune, as well as amphibians, bird nestlings and eggs and small mammals. • The related California mountain kingsnake (*L. zonata*) has a red stripe within the black, mimicking the coloration of the venomous coral snake (*Micrurus* spp.), which is found only in the eastern U.S. **Where found:** near water and farming areas; oak savannahs, mixed pine-oak woodlands and brushy chaparral; west of the Cascades and in Honey Lake Basin east of the Cascades.

California Whipsnake

Masticophis lateralis

Length: 2½–5 ft

This high strung, energetic snake moves about with its head held high, investigating its surroundings. Quick and agile, offering a challenging race to its pursuers, it preys mainly upon lizards but will not reject other food sources such as insects, snakes, small mammals, frogs, birds and their nestlings. • The underbelly of this snake is yellow, turning a distinct pink under the length of the tail. **Where found:** brushy chaparral of rocky foothills, often along streams; throughout most of California's mountain ranges, reaching its northern ranges in extreme southern Siskiyou County.

Rubber Boa

Charina bottae

Length: 15–30 in

This snake's small, smooth dorsal scales and soft, loose skin give it a rubbery appearance. It is sometimes called the "two-headed snake" because its head and the tip of its tail have the same thickness and coloring. • Like most constrictors, the rubber boa is an excellent climber and strangles its prey, which includes lizards, amphibians, birds and small mammals. Its defensive posture is to roll up into a ball, hiding its head. **Where found:** under logs or rocks; in grassy openings among trees in wooded areas and coniferous forests at lower elevations throughout Northern California.

Sharp-tailed Snake

Contia tenuis

Length: 8–18 in

A sharp spine on the tip of its tail gives this small snake its name. Herpetologists studying this snake have indicated that the spine is used as an anchor in the soil while the snake pulls at a resting slug or worm that it is preying upon. The sharp-tailed snake's diet is almost exclusively made up of small slugs and sometimes worms, thus damp areas are the most suitable habitat for it. A good time to look for one of these snakes is after a warm rain. **Where found:** oak woodlands, coniferous forests, brushy chaparral and grassy savannahs from sea level to 4000 ft.

FISH

Fish are ectothermic vertebrates that live in the water, have streamlined bodies covered in scales, and possess fins and gills. A fundamental feature of fish is the serially repeated set of vertebrae and segmented muscles that allow the animal to move from side to side, propelling it through the water. A varying number of fins (depending on the species) further aid the fish to swim and navigate. Most fish are oviparous and lay eggs that are fertilized externally. Eggs are either produced in vast quantities and scattered, or they are laid in a spawning nest (redd) under rocks or logs. Parental care may be present in the defence of such a nest or territory. Spawning can involve migrating vast distances back to freshwater spawning grounds after spending 2 – 3 years in the ocean.

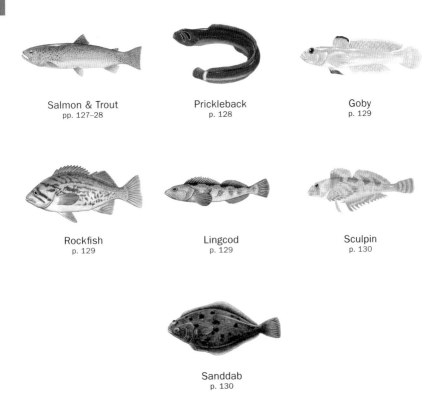

Salmon & Trout
pp. 127–28

Prickleback
p. 128

Goby
p. 129

Rockfish
p. 129

Lingcod
p. 129

Sculpin
p. 130

Sanddab
p. 130

Chinook Salmon

Oncorhynchus tshawytscha

Length: 2½–5 ft

The Chinook salmon is the largest
North American salmon, weighing up to 126 lb,
making it a popular sport fish. Most salmon spend a year in freshwater and then
travel up to 900 mi to the Pacific Ocean. After 3 years in the ocean, they return to
their place of birth to spawn and then die. • During spawning, males have a slightly
humped back and a hooked jaw, and they turn dark red to black with a greenish
head. **Where found:** saltwater and freshwater habitats from San Francisco Bay north.

Cutthroat Trout

Oncorhynchus clarki

Length: 8–12 in

Named for the red streaking in
the skin under the lower jaw, cutthroat
trout seen in the water can be mistakenly identified
as the similar-looking rainbow trout. The cutthroat's reddish belly and throat
become brighter during spawning. Females excavate spawning nests (redds) with
their tails in late spring or early summer. • There are 3 native subspecies of cutthroat
trout in California. Some populations are coastal, others are freshwater residents
and some travel between the brackish estuaries and the freshwater tributaries.
Where found: saltwater and freshwater habitats from the Eel River drainage north.

Rainbow Trout

Oncorhynchus mykiss

Length: 7½–18 in

There are different life history
behaviors between populations of
rainbow trout in California. Coastal rainbow trout
are also called steelhead trout and spend a portion of their life cycle in the ocean,
returning to freshwater streams to spawn. Summer steelhead trout enter their
natal rivers in spring or summer and hold there until winter or spring, when they
spawn; other steelhead trout enter the river in fall or winter and spawn in late
winter or early spring. Coastal streams may support both steelhead and freshwater residents. **Where found:** saltwater and freshwater habitats; entire coast and
inland to the Sacramento–San Joaquin system.

Brook Trout

Salvelinus fontinalis

Length: 10 in

Colorful and feisty, the brook trout is a prized sport fish introduced from eastern North America. It is known to interbreed with other species of trout, and strong management practices must be put into place to protect native fish. • Brook trout are a type of char. They are fall spawners and are capable of reproducing in the substrate of high mountain lakes, whereas other trout species require clean gravel beds in flowing water. **Where found:** freshwater habitats; widespread throughout mountain lakes.

Brown Trout

Salmo trutta

Length: 18–35 in

The brown trout's large size and adaptability have made it a popular sport fish throughout the world. Like most other trout, it spawns in fall and eats aquatic invertebrates. A brown trout will also eat the occasional amphibian or small mammal that ventures into the water. Its color ranges from golden brown to olive. • This species was introduced to the United States in 1893 from Europe. **Where found:** freshwater habitats; streams, ponds, lakes and reservoirs.

Black Prickleback

Xiphister atropurpureus

Length: up to 12 in

Although it looks and acts similar to an eel, the black prickleback is not a true eel. It often slithers out of the water under rocks and seaweed, able to breathe air as long as it is relatively moist. It can stay out of water for up to 10 hours, possibly more. • The black prickleback spawns off the central California coast from February to April. The male guards the nest of 738–4070 eggs. **Where found:** saltwater habitats; close to rocky shores with algal cover; lower intertidal and shallow subtidal zones down to depths of 26 ft; small individuals are common in tide pools; under rocks and in gravel areas. **Also known as:** black blenny.

Blackeye Goby

Rhinogobiops nicholsii

Length: up to 6 in

Frequently seen by sport divers,
gobies have interesting colors and pat-
terns and large eyes. The blackeye goby is less colorful than many other gobies,
but it has distinctive black, bulbous eyes that contrast with its pale body. A black
border to the dorsal fin (and the pectoral fin of breeding males) is a diagnostic
feature. • It nests from April to September, laying 500–3000 eggs over the spawning season, and is very territorial against other blackeye gobies. **Where found:**
saltwater habitats; sand- and mud-bottomed waters near rocky areas and reefs
and in bays as well as in deep waters. **Also known as:** *Coryphopterus nicholsi.*

Blue Rockfish

Sebastes mystinus

Length: up to 21 in

Significant numbers of these fish
are claimed by sport fishing each year;
their wild predators include seals and sea lions.
To reduce predation, female rockfish carry their eggs
internally until just before they are ready to hatch. • Blue rockfish are sometimes
found in large groups feeding on jellyfish, smaller fish and crustaceans. They can
also be found among rocky reefs, where they are a popular subject of underwater
photography. Their sedentary behavior makes it seem like they actually pose for
the camera. • More than 50 species of rockfish live in Californian waters. **Where
found:** saltwater habitats; rocky reefs in both shallow and deep waters; kelp beds.

Lingcod

Ophiodon elongatus

Length: up to 5 ft

The largest lingcod on record in California is 41½ lb, while in British Columbia,
Canada, one massive individual weighed in at 105 lb. It is a highly prized sport
fish and popular with both humans and sea-lions for eating. • This spiny,
unfriendly looking fish is very territorial. Males vigilantly guard nests containing
egg masses 2 ft across. **Where found:** saltwater habitats; seasonal migration
between shallow and deep waters to 1500 ft. *Adult:* rocky reefs and kelp. *Juvenile:*
sandy or muddy bays.

Tidepool Sculpin

Oligocottus maculosus

Length: 3½ in

Sculpins are famous for their looks—they're so ugly that they're cute. Bulging eyes, fat, wide lips, roughly textured skin with mottled coloration and dorsal spines add up to one visually impressive fish. • An individual tidepool sculpin tends to select one particular tide pool to call home and will return to it if displaced. **Where found:** saltwater habitats; sheltered intertidal areas; tide pools.

Pacific Sanddab

Citharichthys sordidus

Length: up to 16 in

The Pacific sanddab is a type of flatfish that hides in the sand on the seafloor. Its flat body and cryptic coloration keep this fish almost invisible with only a thin layer of sand atop it. • Although born with an eye on either side of its head, the Pacific sanddab spends its life lying on its right side, resulting in both its eyes shifting to the left (top) side of its body (occasionally an individual will lie to the other side). • It is a highly sought-after fish commercially as well as by anglers. **Where found:** saltwater habitats; soft, sandy ocean floors.

INVERTEBRATES

More than 95% of all animal species on the planet are invertebrates, and there are thousands of invertebrate species in Northern California. The few mentioned in this guide are frequently encountered and easily recognizable. Invertebrates can be found in a variety of habitats and are an important part of most ecosystems. They provide food for a variety of land and marine animals. Terrestrial invertebrates also play an important role in the pollination of plants and aid in the decay process.

Seashells
pp. 133–34

Sea Slug
p. 134

Sea Cucumber
p. 135

Sea Stars
p. 135

Sand Dollars & Sea
Urchins, p. 136

Anemones, Coral &
Sponges, pp. 136–37

Jellyfish
p. 138

Octopus
p. 138

Crustaceans
pp. 139–40

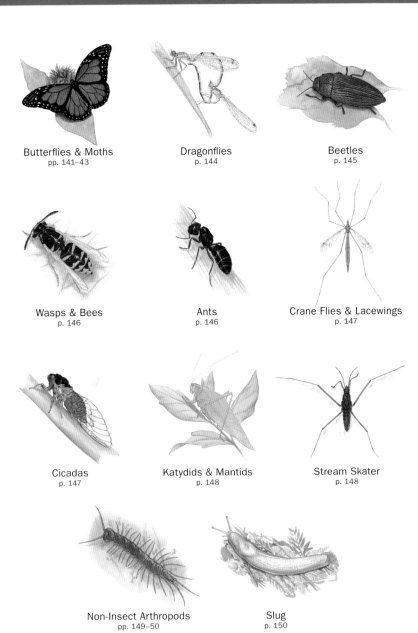

Butterflies & Moths
pp. 141–43

Dragonflies
p. 144

Beetles
p. 145

Wasps & Bees
p. 146

Ants
p. 146

Crane Flies & Lacewings
p. 147

Cicadas
p. 147

Katydids & Mantids
p. 148

Stream Skater
p. 148

Non-Insect Arthropods
pp. 149–50

Slug
p. 150

Giant Owl Limpet

Lottia gigantea

Length: up to 4½ in

"Giant" is a relative term, but this little limpet does push its weight around, bullying away smaller limpets. It stakes out its territory of about 1 ft² and will literally push other species of limpets out. Once it has cleared its space of pesky neighbors, it has a fine garden of algae to sustain itself on. When not grazing, the giant owl limpet positions itself within a groove that it carves into a rock, which it then tightly clamps itself against. **Where found:** on exposed rocks in heavy surf areas between high- and low-tide lines.

Black Abalone

Haliotis cracherodii

Length: 6 in

There are several species of abalone in our local coastal waters, and most are highly prized commercially and have been overharvested. To prevent over-exploitation, several restrictions have been put in place to protect them. Red abalones (*H. rufescens*) are the largest and most prized. Black abalones are edible but are not fished commercially and thus, luckily, remain fairly abundant. • Black abalones feed mainly on large brown algae. • Never cut an abalone off its rock; they are hemophiliacs and will bleed to death if cut. **Where found:** deep crevices in rocks between high- and low-tide lines to water 20 ft deep.

Black Tegula

Tegula funebralis

Length: 1 in

These snails are some of the most abundant on the Pacific Coast. Large individuals are known to live 20–30 years. They take advantage of sloped substrates to flee predators such as sea stars by pulling inside their shells and rolling away. • Empty black tegula shells are a favorite home acquisition of hermit crabs. **Where found:** on rocky shores between high- and low-tide lines. **Also known as:** turban tegula.

California Mussel

Mytilus californianus

Length: 10 in

California mussels are the most conspicuous and abundant animals on our shores. They are predominant in the upper tidal zone and occur in massive growths. Mussels are capable of limited locomotion but rarely move from their practically permanent position; they attach to a substrate by byssal threads produced by their foot. • Sea stars, crabs, shorebirds and sea otters are among their top predators, but the supreme enthusiast for this tasty mollusk is human. **Where found:** on rocks, wharf pilings and unprotected shores; from well above the low-tide line to water 80 ft deep.

Lined Chiton

Tonicella lineate

Length: 2 in

The gorgeous lined chiton sports an array of fashionable shells typically mottled reddish brown as a background and decorated with zigzag lines patterned across it in colors varying from light and dark reds to blues or browns to black or white. The fleshy girdle that surrounds the 8-sectioned plate of armor (chitons are the only mollusk with jointed shells) is usually greenish or yellowish. **Where found:** on rocks covered with coralline algae; underneath purple sea urchins; from the low-tide line to depths of 180 ft.

Sea Lemon

Anisodoris nobilis

Length: 10 in

A type of nudibranch, sea lemons are poor swimmers; instead, they crawl along the ocean floor with a strong, suction-like foot common to all slug species. • The sea lemon feeds entirely upon sponges. It has a fruity (lemony according to some) scent that is apparently repellant to predators. • The sea lemon has 2 antenna-like rhinophores at its anterior end, a circular, many-branched cluster of gills on the posterior end and is covered in short, rounded tubercles everywhere in between. **Where found:** on pilings, around docks and on rocks below the low-tide line. **Also known as:** noble Pacific doris.

Red Sea Cucumber

Cucumaria miniata

Length: 10 in

Typically bright red, but also orange, pink or purple, this long, smooth, highly tentacled sea cucumber nestles in crevices and under rocks within moving water currents. It has 10 main retractable tentacles of equal length, each highly branched at the ends, and 5 rows of tube feet along its length. • Sea cucumbers are detritivores, feeding on dead and decaying organic material—in California they feed mainly on kelp shed. • As a defense mechanism, and no doubt effectively repulsive, sea cucumbers can spit out their guts and regenerate them. **Where found:** near the low-tide line and in shallow depths in circulating waters from north to central California.

Bat Star

Patiria miniata

Radius: 6–8 in

Bat stars are the most abundant sea stars on the West Coast. This species is highly variable in color—from reddish orange to purple to green, often with mottled patterns—and form, with 5 (sometimes 4–9) short, thick arms. • Sea stars feed upon bivalves, wrapping around them and forcing them out of their shells, and will scavenge dead fish. Their predators are other sea stars, mollusks and crustaceans, but these are often deterred by the bat star's distasteful chemical secretions. **Where found:** kelp forests; on rocks or sand from the low-tide line to depths of 960 ft.

Ochre Sea Star

Pisaster ochraceus

Radius: 10 in

Beautiful yellow, orange, brown, reddish or purple ochre sea stars often suffer from overcollection by beachcombers who unfortunately do not realize that this color will be lost once the sea star dies and dries up. • Ochre sea stars are an important, keystone predatory species whose absence in an ecosystem causes visible shifts in the numbers, types and dominances of other species. This sea star is abundant on beds of mussels, its favored prey, and is preyed upon by gulls and sea otters. **Where found:** intertidal areas; wave-washed, rocky shores at the low-tide line.

Eccentric Sand Dollar

Dendraster excentricus

Radius: 1½ in

Beachcombers are most familiar with this sand dollar as a smooth, spineless, gray specimen with a 5-petaled flower design in the center of its surface. In its living form, it is furry in appearance, and its color varies from light lavender-gray to brown or reddish brown to dark purple-black. • Eccentric sand dollars colonize sandy ocean floors, stabilizing the strata. In rough waters, they will bury themselves under the sand for protection. • Sand dollars are closely related to sea urchins. **Where found:** sandy bottoms of sheltered bays and open coasts; from the low-tide line to depths of 130 ft.

Purple Sea Urchin

Strongylocentrotus purpuratus

Radius: 2 in without spines

In large populations, the purple sea urchin and the red sea urchin (*S. franciscanus*) are capable of overgrazing and destroying the important kelp forests off the coast of California, a situation that a healthy population of sea otters, the urchin's main predator, keeps in check. • The sea urchin is a delicacy of Japanese cuisine, increasingly popular in California's sushi restaurants. It is also eaten fresh from the shell, much like an oyster, at fishing ports and wharves. • Adult purple sea urchins are a vivid purple, but the juveniles are green. **Where found:** from the low-tide line and rocky shores into kelp forests in waters up to 300 ft deep.

Aggregating Anemone

Anthopleura elegantissima

Height: *Aggregating individuals:* 6 in; *Solitary individuals:* 20 in
Width: *Aggregating individuals:* 3 in; *Solitary individuals:* 10 in

This sea anemone has 5 rings of tentacles with tips varying in delicate colors of pink, lavender and blue. The aggregating form is in fact a colony of clones created by the "founding" anemone, which divides itself in a form of asexual reproduction. These clones tolerate proximity to each other because they are not competing genetically. If a genetically different individual was in proximity, they would lash out with their tentacles, wounding or killing it. Their toxins are completely benign to their clones. **Where found:** rock walls, boulders or pilings from intertidal to low-tide zones.

Giant Green Anemone

Anthopleura xanthogrammica

Height: 12 in
Width: 10 in

The giant green anemone is a solitary giant but is not antisocial. Often within tentacle-tip distance to another anemone, it makes contact every once in a while as if to reassure itself that is it not alone. • Its green column varies to brown, and the thick, short, tapered tentacles vary from green to blue to white in rows of 6 or more. The green coloring is enhanced by a symbiotic relationship with green algae, from which the anemone obtains photosynthetic by-products. **Where found:** exposed coastlines; on rocks, seawalls and pilings in tide pools and to depths of more than 50 ft.

Orange Cup Coral

Balanophyllia elegans

Height: ½ in
Width: ½ in

This is the only stony coral in the intertidal zone of the Pacific Coast from British Columbia to Baja California. Stony coral has a stony, cup-shaped skeleton in which the base of the animal is set, and 36 long, tapered, translucent tentacles reach out and contract back within the skeleton. The tentacles have masses of stinging cells dotted along them, so do not be tempted to touch this lovely, bright orange beauty. The fluorescent pigment is bright even at depths of 30 ft or more. **Where found:** shaded waters such as under ledges and boulders from the low-tide line down to depths of 70 ft; all along the coast.

Purple Sponge

Haliclona permollis

Height: 1½ in
Width: 36 in

Looking like a bubblegum-colored lava spill, this encrusting sponge pours itself over rocks and within tide pools. Its smooth, soft form seems to bubble with little raised volcanoes up to ¼ in higher than the surface of the sponge. • Sponges reproduce either by budding (a tip is released or breaks off and regenerates upon attachment to a new site) or by releasing tiny clusters of cells that germinate on a new site. Sponges are also capable of sexual reproduction, releasing sperm into the water that then fertilizes eggs in another sponge; the larvae swim to a new site, attach and develop into a tiny sponge. **Where found:** sheltered waters from the intertidal zone to depths of 20 ft.

Moon Jellyfish

Aurelia aurita

Radius: 7½ in

This ethereal, whitish to translucent medusa is a favorite food of the leatherback sea turtle but not a favored acquaintance of swimmers and snorkelers—a jellyfish can give a painful sting, but it also releases polyps in the water that are very difficult to see but easily felt. The sting may cause a slight rash or itching for several hours. • The moon jellyfish has 8 lobes fringed by numerous short tentacles and 4 long, oral arms, also with frilly margins. **Where found:** floats near the surface just offshore and often washes up on beaches during high tide or after a storm.

Red Octopus

Octopus rubescens

Armspread: up to 18 in

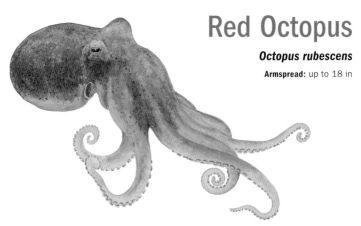

Octopi are extremely advanced invertebrates, possessing many clever behaviors that are a constant source of entertainment for divers and snorkelers; their ability to squirt screens of ink and change the color and texture of their skin to camouflage themselves are among the most impressive. Their camouflaging skills, however, make them challenging to identify. The red octopus is, in fact, often sandy beige to blend in with the sand outside its den, which is noticeable by the deposits of debris from its many lobster (and other invertebrate) dinners. **Where found:** sandy habitats in shallow waters close to shore out to depths of 600 ft.

Giant Acorn Barnacle

Balnus nubilis

Radius: up to 2 in

We typically see this barnacle closed, but, though rarely and sometimes not for months at a time, when it feeds, long, feathery plumes reach out from the top of the barnacle shell to filter bits of organic matter from the water. • This barnacle must remain almost continuously covered by water or it will easily desiccate. • Capable of sexual reproduction yet immobile, this animal has the largest penis-to-body-size ratio in the animal kingdom so that the male can reach his mate. **Where found:** rocky shores and exposed coasts; lower intertidal areas with continuous water cover; subtidal to depths of 300 ft.

Barred Shrimp

Heptacarpus pugettensis

Length: up to 1 in

Heptacarpus species are the "broken-back" shrimps, named for the distinctive kink in their backs. There are many species in quite high numbers along our coast, but they are not often noticeable as they lay motionless in bright daylight hours, their translucent coloring blending into the substrate. Disturb still tidepool waters and watch them scurry. **Where found:** from the low-tide line to depths of 50 ft.

Dungeness Crab

Cancer magister

Length: 6½ in

These crabs are the most sought-after species for commercial harvest on the Pacific Coast south of Alaska. Dungeness crabs are usually only found in water around 100 ft deep, but they come to shallow water to molt their shells, which do not grow with the crabs as they do in other species with exoskeletons. The molted shells often wash up onto the beach. **Where found:** on sand bottoms from the low-tide line to water more than 300 ft deep.

Purple Shore Crab

Hemigrapsus nudus

Length: 2 in

The purple shore crab scuttles sideways about rocky shorelines scavenging animal matter and grazing on the film of algae growing on the rocks. It hides under rocks and burrows under mud for shelter and can remain dry for extended periods without desiccating. **Where found:** open, rocky shores; among seaweeds in shallow, protected waters.

Blue-handed Hermit Crab

Pagurus samuelis

Length: ¾ in

Hermit crabs do not produce their own shells, and only the front portion of their bodies is armored; they must protect the soft regions of their bodies by acquiring discarded snail shells. The black tegula shell is one of the preferred shells for this little crab to use as a home. If the crab outgrows its current shell or finds a more suitable and otherwise unoccupied one, it will relocate. **Where found:** permanent tide pools of the intertidal zone.

Western Tiger Swallowtail

Papilio rutulus

Wingspan: 3¼–3½ in

The "tail" of the swallowtail is defensive. If a bird attacks, it will grab at this extension, sparing the butterfly's body. This butterfly is often seen with the lower half of its wings missing, implying that the strategy must indeed work. • There are several species of swallowtail in California with various colorations, but the western tiger never seems go unnoticed or without a compliment from its observer. • The caterpillar is also stunning, sporting a smooth, green body with bright yellow and blue eyespots at one end. It feeds upon poplar trees. **Where found:** along watercourses and in gardens.

Monarch

Danaus plexippus

Wingspan: 3¾ in

The regal monarch is California's most famous butterfly, known for its wide distribution and incredible migration. Millions of monarchs overwinter as adults in the mountain forests of southern California and Mexico. With warmer temperatures, adults migrate northward, laying eggs in patches of milkweed plants. These eggs quickly develop into adults, which continue north as far as the Canadian Rockies. • Toxic compounds in the milkweed make this insect unpalatable to birds, and the birds remember the coloration of the monarch to avoid it in future. Many butterflies mimic the monarch's coloration to deter the same predators. **Where found:** milkweed patches and flower meadows.

Spring Azure

Celastrina argiolus

Wingspan: 1–1¼ in

This dainty, blue butterfly is one of the first butterflies to announce the arrival of spring. It feeds on the buds and flowers of spring blooms on mountain shrubs. An adult lives for only 1–2 weeks, in which time it must breed and lay its eggs. The larvae often develop on the leaves of dogwood and cherry trees and may be tended to and protected by ants for the sweet "honeydew" that they produce. **Where found:** from lush valley bottoms to high alpine meadows.

Clouded Sulphur, Orange Sulphur

Colias philodice, C. eurytheme

Wingspan: 1½–2 in

Differing from each other mainly in color, which varies from yellow to orange, the many sulphur species are all very tricky to tell apart. • Like all other butterflies, sulphurs play a vital role in pollinating many wild plants. Attracted to flowers by their brilliantly colored petals, butterflies obtain nectar with a long, coilable proboscis and meanwhile are sprinkled with fine, sticky pollen, which they carry to the next plant. **Where found:** meadows, fields and vegetated roadsides; from low-elevation valleys to subalpine areas.

California Dogface

Colias eurydice

Wingspan: 2½ in

The official state insect of California is a beautiful butterfly with an undeservingly ugly name attributed to what supposedly looks like a poodle head on each upper wing. • This butterfly is a type of sulphur, a genus in which purple is an uncommon color. Most male sulphurs have ultraviolet wing scales that reflect color invisible to the human eye but visible and attractive to female sulphurs. These scales on the male California dogface have simply shifted in hue and reentered our visual spectrum to impress us as well as the female California dogface. **Where found:** foothills of the Sierra Nevada and Coast ranges.

California Tortoiseshell

Nymphalis californica

Wingspan: 2½ in

The population of these butterflies fluctuates annually, but when numbers are high, their migration can be quite spectacular. California tortoiseshells, named for their similarity in color to the polished shells of hawksbill sea turtles, migrate between higher mountain elevations in summer and lower elevations in fall. In winter, they seek shelter under the bark of trees or within woodpiles and await spring. **Where found:** wooded areas throughout Northern California.

California Silkmoth

Hyalophora euryalus

Wingspan: 4 in

This spectacular member of the family of giant silkworms is fairly common in California and is always an impressive sight. • The silk from North American silkworms was once considered for commercial use, but the quality does not match that of their Asian counterparts, so the venture was abandoned.
• California silkworms use their silk to make cocoons. When the moth emerges from the pupae, it lacks a mouth and thus does not feed, but survives on its bodily reserves alone for approximately 1 week. **Where found:** shrubby areas throughout Northern California.

Snowberry Clearwing

Hemaris diffinis

Wingspan: 1½ in

This bizarre little insect often fools people into thinking that it is a small hummingbird by the way it hovers around flowers. Its long proboscis, furred body and handsome coloring warrant a closer inspection to affirm that is indeed a moth, actually a member of the sphinx moth family. • Active in the daytime, unusual for a moth, it feeds among the flowers much like a butterfly; its caterpillar feeds on a variety of forest plants. **Where found:** widespread throughout Northern California. **Also known as:** hummingbird moth, bumblebee moth.

California Tent Caterpillar Moth

Malacosoma californicum

Wingspan: 1½ in

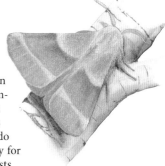

Known more infamously for its caterpillar, this species is seldom recognized in its moth form. It is a simple, brown, furry moth that lays its eggs in a large mass from which the caterpillars hatch. They remain with their siblings in a furry cluster, wrapping themselves up in silk "tents" during the day to hide from predators and foraging on leaves at night. In years when their numbers are high, these caterpillars can do a lot of damage to trees, but they are important prey for many birds and insects. **Where found:** deciduous forests.

Boreal Bluet

Enallagma boreale

Length: 1¼ in

Nearly every pond or lake will host this familiar blue damselfly. The female may sometimes be green or yellow, but the male is always blue. Several other species of bluet are also found in our area and are quite difficult to tell apart. To distinguish a damselfly from a dragonfly, however, notice that damselflies are thin, and all 4 of their wings are similar in shape and are (usually) folded up over their backs. **Where found:** among reeds in ponds and lakes.

California Spreadwing

Archilestes californica

Length: 2–2¼ in

As an exception to the rule about how dragonflies and damselflies posture their wings, this damselfly assumes the dragonfly position, thus giving it the name "spreadwing." This species does not have spectacular coloring, but as an individual ages, it becomes covered in a waxy powder called pruinose that is very much like the waxiness of a plum or prune. Specialists theorize that pruinose adds to the reflectivity of the ultraviolet signals that this insect uses in courtship. **Where found:** near slow-flowing streams.

Variegated Meadowhawk

Sympetrum corruptum

Length: 1½ in

Like so much of nature, there is still a lot left to learn when it comes to variegated meadowhawks. These widespread dragonflies stage a mass migration on the West Coast in fall. They are observed heading south, but it is yet unknown where they travel to, where they came from prior to congregating *en masse*, or even what triggers them to know when to do so. Some experts are studying whether fall wind patterns give them environmental clues as to their travel date. **Where found:** ponds and lakes; prefers stagnant waters.

Pacific Tiger Beetle

Cicindela oregona

Length: ½ in

The Pacific tiger beetle is not the most colorful of its kind, but it is impressive nonetheless with its powerful jaws and fast movements. It is common, but you have to have a quick eye to see one before it dashes off to hide. • This beetle preys on insects and can be seen on the prowl either hunting for its dinner or searching for a mate. **Where found:** moist sand and gravel alongside rivers and lakes; widespread.

Golden Jewel Beetle

Buprestis aurulenta

Length: ¾ in

With their brilliant metallic coloring, jewel beetles rarely go unnoticed; the golden jewel beetle is one of the most attractive of its family in Northern California. Other members of this family of wood-borers are found in the tropics and are sometimes made into jewelry. • This insect thrives in the heat of summer and in forests with plenty of dead, decaying wood, where its larvae live. **Where found:** coniferous forests.

Convergent Ladybug

Hippodamia convergens

Length: ¼ in

There are several species of ladybug, all distinguishable from each other by their size, number of spots and coloration. Some ladybugs are not even red. • They emerge from the pupae and do not change their size or number of spots as they age. • Ladybugs feed ravenously on aphids. They can be bought in garden centers to put in a garden with aphid problems; they will have a significant impact, especially in a greenhouse. Once released, most will fly away. **Where found:** open areas and hilltops in spring and fall.

Yellow Jackets

Vespula spp.

Length: ½–¾ in

Amazing engineers of paper architecture, yellow jackets chew on bark or wood and mix it with saliva to make the pulp. Large sheets of paper line the nest in which 6-sided paper chambers hold the larvae. Different types of wood create swirls of color, grays and browns, inadvertently adding some artistic style to the structure. The nest can reach the size of a basketball by the end of summer; only the queen, however, will survive winter—the only safe time of year to get a close-up look at a wasp nest without being stung by one of the architects. **Where found:** widespread in Northern California; nests in high branches or in abandoned animal burrows. **Also known as:** paper wasp, hornet.

Bumble Bees

Bombus spp.

Length: ¼–¾ in

Bees have long inspired our admiration and appreciation; throughout history, the image of the bee appears on ancient coins, in Masonic, Mormon, Pagan, Egyptian, Jewish and Greek symbology, as an icon of royalty in Sudan, Niger, France and India, as a personal emblem adopted by Napoleon Bonaparte, as a sacred feminine symbol of the Cult of Athena and as an embodiment of the goddess Venus—just to name a few examples! **Where found:** clearings and meadows wherever there are flowering plants.

Carpenter Ants

Camponotus spp.

Length: ½ in

Similar but unrelated to termites, carpenter ants bore through wood to construct their homes in trees and sometimes in our wooden homes as well. Watch for a pile of sawdust in either case. • These are the largest ants in our area, and they are preyed upon by our largest woodpeckers, pileated woodpeckers. • Carpenter ants do not sting as do other ant species, but their powerful, wood-chewing jaws are capable of a strong bite. **Where found:** forested areas.

Giant Crane Flies

Holorusia spp.

Length: up to 1½ in

These innocent insects are not giant mosquitoes or garden harvestmen ("daddy longlegs") but very benign and harmless crane flies. Giant crane flies do not bite, and their larvae only scavenge in soil and rotting logs. • The crane is an appropriate analogy to these long-legged creatures, which are more comfortable in the forest than when they accidentally find themselves inside your house. **Where found:** forested areas.

Green Lacewings

Chrysopa spp.

Length: ½ in

Lacewings are frequent visitors to your garden, where their lime green bodies are camouflaged by the light green foliage of young plants. • These insects have elegant, filigreed wings, hence the name "lacewing," large golden eyes and, if you pick one up, you will notice they produce an odd scent. • Both the adults and larvae of these beneficial insects feed on aphids. **Where found:** shrubby or forested areas and gardens; widespread.

Cicada

Family Cicadidae

Length: ¾ in

Take a walk in sagebrush country in mid-summer, and the fields will be resonating with the music of the male cicada. A loud, prolonged, dry, rattling buzz is the sound made by a vibration in the insect's abdomen. • The larvae live underground for years, feeding on roots until they finally emerge one summer, ready to make some noise. • The species in the West do not often reproduce to the infesting numbers that can famously occur in the East, nor are these insects locusts, which are a type of grasshopper. **Where found:** dry, forested or shrubby areas, particularly in sagebrush country in the northeast of the state.

Angular-winged Katydid

Microcentrum rhombofolium

Length: 2½ in

"You are what you eat" is an apt expression for this leaf eater, which looks like a walking green leaf. Katydids use this plant mimicry to hide from predators, and in some parts of the world, other species of katydid even have fake chew marks or decay marks, adding further believability to their leaf-like wings. **Where found:** open, vegetated areas; recently colonized in Northern California from eastern North America.

California Mantid

Stagomomantis californica

Length: 2½ in

No matter what color—green, yellow or brown—a mantid is always admired. Its slow, deliberate movements are analogous to tai chi martial arts movements, and this insect's ability to move its "neck" to observe a passing object or our own human gaze is somehow human-like. **Where found:** dry, shrubby areas in the Sacramento Valley.

Stream Skater

Aquaricus remigis

Length: ¾ in

Surface tension on water along with the body shape of this insect allows the stream skater to walk, or skate, on water. Its legs are water repellant but also long and far-reaching, thus distributing the skater's weight over a large area. • Like a diligent pool cleaner, the stream skater prowls the water's surface for dead or drowning bugs, which it quickly consumes. **Where found:** streams and small rivers.

Garden Centipedes

Lithobius spp.

Length: up to 1¼ in

A centipede moves its many legs very quickly, but if you manage to see one sitting still, you can count 1 set of legs per body segment—significantly less than 100 feet, as the name suggests. • This predator has venomous fangs with which it subdues its prey. It is not dangerous to people but should nevertheless be avoided, especially by small children. • Centipedes require a moist environment to survive and will quickly desiccate if they find their way into a house. **Where found:** under moist debris or cover in gardens and forests.

Clown Millipede

Harapaphe haydeniana

Length: 1¾ in

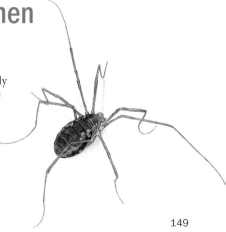

Although it has twice as many legs (2 sets per body segment) as the centipede, the millipede moves only half as fast—actually quite slowly. Because it feeds upon plants and detritus, the clown millipede does not need to move quickly to catch a meal. Its main defense against animals such as birds and lizards that want to prey upon it is to curl up into a ball and produce cyanide, which has an odor that deters would-be predators. Some people compare the scent produced by the millipede to that of almonds. **Where found:** forested areas with Douglas-fir. **Also know as:** cyanide millipede.

Garden Harvestmen

Order Opiliones

Length: _Body:_ ¼ in

Garden harvestmen are also commonly referred to as "daddy longlegs" or are incorrectly referred to as spiders. They primarily scavenge dead bugs, but they can hunt small insects. They do not bite and are altogether harmless. • Harvestmen cannot produce silk for spinning webs **Where found:** dark, moist habitats.

California Ebony Tarantula

Aphonopelma eutylenum

Length: up to 1¾ in

This secretive spider lives in crevices and burrows in grassy, open areas, but the male will venture out during the fall breeding season in search of a mate. • The California ebony tarantula is slow moving and prefers to wait for an insect to unwarily walk past the entrance of its burrow, where the spider can grab it. • This tarantula's venom is not dangerous to humans, and it is unlikely to bite in defense; rather, it will use its legs to flick the hairs from its abdomen at an attacker. The hairs are barbed and very irritating to the skin. **Where found:** open areas; chaparral and grasslands.

Western Black Widow

Latrodectus hesperus

Length: *Male:* up to ¼ in; *Female:* up to ½ in

Not known for its web-making skills, the black widow makes a disorganized mass of web in the abandoned burrows of small mammals. If seen out of hiding, the western black widow is easy to identify by its shiny, large, black body with a red hourglass on the underside of the abdomen. • The bite of a black widow is dangerous and best avoided. • The female really does often eat the male after mating, but the black widow is not the only spider to do so. **Where found:** dry, well-drained areas throughout Northern California.

Yellow-orange Banana Slug

Ariolimax columbianus

Length: up to 10 in

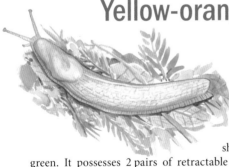

The largest slug in North America and second largest in the world, the yellow-orange banana slug often looks quite rightly like a banana on the forest floor, but it can also vary in shade or be mottled with brown and green. It possesses 2 pairs of retractable tentacles; the longer ones sense the brightness of light, and the shorter ones sense smell. • This slug lives 1–7 years. It is an important forest floor decomposer, scavenging organic debris and favoring mushrooms. **Where found:** under logs or debris on moist forest floors in northwestern California.

PLANTS

Plants belong to the Kingdom Plantae. They are autotrophic, which means that they produce their own food from inorganic materials through a process called photosynthesis. Plants are the basis of all food webs. They supply oxygen to the atmosphere, modify climate, and create and hold down soil. They disperse their seeds and pollen through carriers such as wind or animals. Fossil fuels come from ancient deposits of organic matter—largely that of plants. In this book, plants are separated into 3 categories: trees, shrubs and herbs and other plants.

TREES

Trees are long-lived, woody plants that are normally taller than 16 ft. There are 2 types of trees: coniferous and broadleaf. Conifers, or cone-bearers, have needles or small, scale-like leaves. Most conifers are evergreens, but larches, bald-cypress (*Taxodium distichum*) and dawn redwood (*Metasequoia glyptostroboides*) shed their leaves in winter. Most broadleaf trees lose their leaves in fall, and are known as deciduous trees (meaning "falling off" in Latin). Some exceptions include rhododendrons and several hollies.

Trees are important to a variety of ecosystems. A single tree can provide a home or a food source for many different animals. A group of trees can provide windbreak, camouflage or shelter, hold down soil and control runoff. A forest that is large and diverse in its structure and composition defines the community of species that live within it. Old-growth forest is critical habitat for many species that use the fallen or hollowed out trees as nesting or denning sites. Fallen, decomposing logs also provide habitat for mosses, fungi and invertebrates. The logs eventually completely degrade into nutrient-rich soil. Large forests retain carbon dioxide, an important preventive factor of global warming, and responsibly managed forests can sustain an industry that provides wood products and jobs.

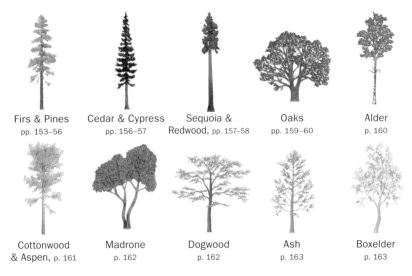

Firs & Pines
pp. 153–56

Cedar & Cypress
pp. 156–57

Sequoia &
Redwood, pp. 157–58

Oaks
pp. 159–60

Alder
p. 160

Cottonwood
& Aspen, p. 161

Madrone
p. 162

Dogwood
p. 162

Ash
p. 163

Boxelder
p. 163

White Fir

Abies concolor

Height: 130–180 ft
Needles: 2–3 in long
Seed cones: 3–5½ in long

Christmas trees are often white fir, with a fragrance that creates nostalgia for the holiday season. Foresters don't often view this tree with the same fondness, because it is shade tolerant and outcompetes sugar pines and incense cedars. In addition, its low-hanging limbs are a fire hazard, inviting small fires to reach up to the canopy and threaten otherwise unreachable trees such as the giant sequoia. • This tree's soft, knotty wood is used commercially only for pulp and cheap construction materials. **Where found:** Sierra Nevada, Klamath and Siskiyou ranges; grows best in the southern Cascades and on the western slopes of the Sierra Nevada. **Also known as:** amabilis fir, Pacific silver fir.

Shore Pine

Pinus contorta

Height: up to 65 ft
Needles: 1–2¾ in long, in pairs
Seed cones: 1–2 in long

Shore pine does indeed grow near the shore and does not merely tolerate but seems to thrive in the salty sea spray and ocean winds, making it fairly common along the immediate coast where most other trees can't survive. This tough climate, however, causes this tenacious tree to grow twisted and stunted. • Native groups used the roots for rope, the bark for splints and the pitch for waterproofing or as a glue. **Where found:** exposed outer-coastal shorelines, dunes, bogs and rocky hilltops. **Also known as:** lodgepole pine (*P. c.* var. *latifolia*), which grows straight and tall, to 130 ft, in its non-coastal range.

Jeffrey Pine

Pinus jeffreyi

Height: up to 180 ft, more typically 100 ft
Needles: 5–11 in long, in 3s
Seed cones: 5½–11½ in long

Jeffrey pine superficially resembles ponderosa pine. The 2 species can be distinguished by smelling the resin: Jeffrey pine resin has a scent similar to lemon or vanilla, whereas ponderosa pine's smells more like turpentine. The sweet scent comes from n-heptane, an unusual and volatile component. Resin distillers back in the 1800s suffered random explosions until they discovered the compound and quickly learned to identify and avoid Jeffrey pines. • Western gray squirrels relish the ripe pine seeds, whereas deer, rabbits, pocket gophers and porcupines eat and destroy the young saplings. **Where found:** dry, cold mountain elevations where other pines suffer; Klamath, northern Coast and eastern Cascade-Sierra ranges.

Sugar Pine

Pinus lambertiana

Height: 175–200 ft
Needles: 2–4½ in long, in bundles of 5
Seed cones: 9¾–19¾ in long

Sugar pine is the largest species of pine and has the longest cones of any conifer. Mature individuals occasionally surpass 500 years of age, with volumes second only to the giant sequoia. Famed naturalist John Muir is noted to have considered the sugar pine the "king of conifers." • This pine gets its name from its sweet sap, which rivals that of maples, though this virtue has been unable to save it from the chainsaw. Sugar pine is heavily harvested beyond its regrowth potential. **Where found:** wide range of soil conditions typically associated with conifer-hardwood forests; Sierra Nevada, Cascade and Coast ranges from sea level to 10,000 ft.

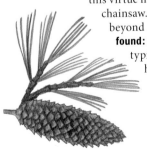

Ponderosa Pine

Pinus ponderosa

Height: 33–130 ft
Needles: 4–10 in long, in bundles of 3
Seed cones: 3–5½ in long

These stately pines thrive in areas that are periodically burned. • The straight, cinnamon-colored trunks are distinctive, with black fissures outlining a jigsaw puzzle of thick plates of bark. • Native peoples ground the oil-rich seeds into meal and collected the sweet inner bark in spring, when the sap was running. Large scars can still be seen on some older trees, attesting to people's fondness for this sweet treat. • The cones have thick, dull brown scales tipped with a stiff prickle. **Where found:** mountains and foothills; east of the Sierra Nevada and Cascade ranges. **Also known as:** yellow pine.

Douglas-fir

Pseudotsuga menziesii

Height: 82–130 ft
Needles: ¾–1¼ in long, aromatic, blunt, often flattened, in 2 rows
Seed cones: 2–4 in long

In Native mythology, mice hid in Douglas-fir cones, and their tails and hind legs can still be seen sticking out from under the scales. • The inner bark and seeds were survival foods for Native groups and pioneers; the young, vitamin C–rich needles were used in teas to treat scurvy; and the sugar crystals that form on the tips of the branches on hot days were a rare treat. • This tree is a top timber producer and makes a fragrant Christmas tree, but if left to grow, a Douglas-fir can live for well over 1000 years. **Where found:** moist to very dry sites in the Klamath, Coast and Sierra Nevada ranges as far south as Yosemite. **Also known as:** red fir, Douglas spruce.

Western Hemlock

Tsuga heterophylla

Height: 100–165 ft
Needles: ⅜–¾ in long, flat, blunt, in 2 opposite rows
Seed cones: ⅝–1 in long

These attractive, feathery trees are popular as ornamentals, and the hard, strong, even-grained wood is widely used to make cabinets, moldings and flooring, and also provides lumber, pilings, poles and pulp. • The crushed needles smell like poison-hemlock (*Conium maculatum*), hence the common name. • In subalpine zones, mountain hemlock (*T. mertensiana*) is distinguishable from western hemlock because its cones are 2–3 times longer and the needles grow in a bottlebrush-like arrangement. **Where found:** moist, humid sites along the Coast ranges; western and upper eastern slopes of the Cascades; a component of redwood forests. **Also known as:** Pacific hemlock, West Coast hemlock.

Incense Cedar

Calocedrus decurrens

Height: 60–80 ft, up to 150 ft in the Sierra Nevada
Needles: ⅛–½ in long, scale-like, overlapping
Seed cones: ¾–1½ in long

Although it is resistant to decay and thus desirable for exterior building panels, the most common use of incense cedar wood is in the manufacture of pencils! If not fated to this studious enterprise, this tree is quite long lived—the oldest on record is 542 years old. • Incense cedar is a deciduous conifer, shedding its needles in fall. In dense groves, these trees can produce a couple of thousand pounds of litter per acre per year, providing ample fuel for many California forest fires. Studies show the natural fire cycle to be every 3–11 years. **Where found:** dry, shady sites; Coast, Cascade and Sierra Nevada ranges.

Monterey Cypress

Cupressus macrocarpa

Height: 80 ft
Leaves: evergreen, scale-like, ¾ in long
Seed cones: 1½ in long

Endemic to California's central coast, this tree is a species of conservation concern, considered rare in its range after portions of the Monterey cypress grove on Monterey Peninsula was destroyed for housing developments and golf courses. Where it survives on the harsh coastal fringe, it grows sculptured and distorted by the ceaseless assault of wind and salt water that it endures throughout its 200- to 300-year lifespan. **Where found:** 2 small wild populations near Monterey and Carmel; cultivated and naturalized along other parts of the coast with similar habitat and climate. **Also known as:** macrocarpa (in New Zealand, where it is cultivated and grows up to 130 ft).

Giant Sequoia

Sequoiadendron giganteum

Height: average 250 ft
Leaves: ⅛–½ in long, almost scale-like
Seed cones: 2–3½ in long

Giant sequoias are the world's largest trees in sheer volume, inspiring the largest tree-hugs around their bases. Living 2000–3000 years, the oldest known specimen dated by its stump rings was 3200 years old when it was cut. Living legends include the General Sherman in Sequoia National Park (the most massive at 52,500 ft³, with a trunk base of 109 ft in circumference) and the General Grant in Kings Canyon National Park (the tallest at 310 ft). **Where found:** about 75 groves are scattered along a 260-mi belt, nowhere more than about 15 mi wide, along the western slopes of the Sierra Nevada. **Also known as:** sequoia, bigtree, Sierra redwood.

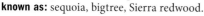

Redwood

Sequoia sempervirens

Height: 300–350 ft
Needles: ½–¾ in long, in 2 lateral rows on the branch, or ¼-in long, scale-like near the cones
Seed cones: ½–1 in long (or slightly longer)

The coastal redwoods are the tallest living species on Earth, with a few giants exceeding 360 ft in height. • Redwoods are extremely efficient photosynthesizers, able to grow even in deep shade. However, in full sunlight (and moist soil), a redwood sapling can grow more than 6 ft in a single season. • Siphoning water up such great heights is an amazing hydrostatic achievement, but redwoods can also create their own rain to quench their dry roots by condensing heavy fog in their canopy. Here, dense mats of vegetative debris act like sponges to also moisten canopy roots that sprout from the branches. • The oldest known redwood is at least 2200 years old. However, because this species can reproduce by suckering, a tree may be genetically identical to a prehistoric parent. • Logging has taken 95% of the virgin coastal redwood forest and remains a daily threat. Protected old-growth redwoods occupy less than 200,000 acres, and the old-growth trees in commercial forests will be harvested within the next few decades. **Where found:** in a coastal strip about 450 mi long and 5–35 mi wide from the extreme southwestern corner of Oregon to southern Monterey County. **Also known as:** coast redwood, California redwood.

Tanoak

Lithocarpus densiflorus

Height: 65–150 ft
Leaves: 4 in long, leathery, toothed margins
Flowers: upright catkins
Fruit: acorns with fringed cups, ¾–1¼ in long, ¾ in diameter

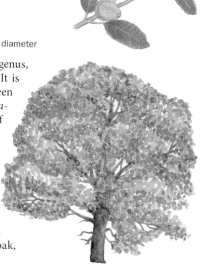

This tree was once classified in the *Quercus* genus, but was given its own genus, *Lithocarpus*. It is believed to be an evolutionary link between the oaks (*Quercus* spp.) and chestnuts (*Castanea* spp.). The flowers resemble those of chestnuts while the fruit is an acorn, a characteristic of oaks. • This genus is typical of southeast Asia. • The leaves are leathery with toothed margins, evergreen and covered in hairs for first few years. • The bark is high in tannins and was used for tanning hides. **Where found:** on the coast and in the Sierra Nevada. **Also known as:** tanbark oak, California chestnut oak, chestnut oak, live oak, peach oak.

California Black Oak

Quercus kelloggii

Height: 30–80 ft
Leaves: 3–8 in long, 2–5 in wide, elliptical with 7 lobes
Flowers: 1½–3 in long
Fruit: acorns, 1–1½ in long, 1–3¾ in diameter

Black oak exceeds all other California oaks in volume, distribution and altitudinal range. It covers more area in California than any other hardwood species and can live up to 500 years. • Many animals including the western gray squirrel and the scrub jay rely on this tree for acorns as food in fall, and mule deer fawn survival rates have been linked to acorn crop abundance. These trees also provide nesting cavities for owls, woodpeckers and squirrels, and den sites for black bears. **Where found:** areas with hot, dry summers and cool, moist winters; foothills and lower mountains, mainly on the west side of the Sierra Nevada. **Also known as:** black oak, Kellogg's oak, *Q. californica.*

California Live Oak

Quercus agrifolia

Height: 30–80 ft
Leaves: 1–2¾ in long, ¾–1½ in wide, spiny-toothed
Flowers: male in pendulous catkins, 2–4 in long; female inconspicuous
Fruit: ovoid acorns, 1–2½ in long, ½ in wide

The name "live oak" simply means that this oak is an evergreen, retaining green leaves and "living" through the winter, though technically it is classified as a red oak. • The acorns of this oak were a staple for Native groups. Charcoal made from the wood was used by the early Spaniards to fire their kilns to make adobe; in later years, the charcoal was used for gunpowder and electric power industries. **Where found:** valleys, slopes, mixed evergreen forests, woodlands; the only oak to grow near the coast; west of the Sierra Nevada from Mendocino County south. **Also known as:** coast live oak.

Red Alder

Alnus rubra

Height: over 80 ft
Leaves: 2–6 in long, broadly elliptical
Flowers: hanging catkins; male catkins 2–4¾ in long; female catkins ¾ in long
Fruit: brownish cones, ¾ in long

This tree gets its name from the red color that develops when the bark is scraped or bruised. • A tip for your next fish barbeque: use red alder wood. It is considered the best for smoking fish, especially salmon. It is also an attractive wood for artistic carvings and bowls, and the tannins in the bark can be used to make a red dye. The bark was used traditionally for a variety of medicinal purposes and was reputed to have antibiotic properties. The ancient Romans treated tumors with alder leaves, which modern scientists have since learned contain the tumor-suppressing compounds betulin and lupeol. **Where found:** low-elevation moist woods, streambanks, floodplains, cleared land.

Black Cottonwood

Populus balsamifera ssp. *trichocarpa*

Height: up to 160 ft
Leaves: 2–6 in
Flowers: catkins, male ¾–1¼ in long, female 1⅝–4 in or longer, on separate trees
Fruit: oval capsules, ¼ in long

This tree is the largest of the American poplars and the largest hardwood in North America. • The young catkins and the sweet inner bark of spring were eaten by many Native groups. Medicinally, the leaves, bark and resins from the sticky, aromatic buds were important for treating many conditions and ailments. The resins are still used today for salves, cough medicines and pain-killers. • The wood is ideal for campfires because it does not crackle and the smoke is less acrid than that of other wood. **Where found:** on moist to wet sites, often on shores; also in foothills to subalpine zones. **Also known as:** balm-of-Gilead, *P. trichocarpa.*

Quaking Aspen

Populus tremuloides

Height: 65–82 ft
Leaves: ¾–3 in long
Flowers: catkins, ¾–4 in long, male and female catkins on separate trees
Fruit: cone-shaped capsules that release many tiny seeds tipped with soft, white hairs

The name "quaking" refers to the way the leaves tremble in the slightest breeze because of the narrow leaf stalks. This is a good way to differentiate quaking aspen from the similar black cottonwood. • Aspen trunks were once used for more romantic purposes such as tipi poles and canoe paddles; today, the wood is primarily harvested for pulp and for making chopsticks. However, it is a preferred wood for sauna benches because it does not splinter, which may not be romantic but is definitely sensible. **Where found:** dry to moist sites in foothills to subalpine zones. **Also known as:** trembling aspen, aspen poplar.

161

Pacific Madrone

Arbutus menziesii

Height: 50–100 ft
Leaves: 2–6 in long
Flowers: ¼ in long, greenish white, sweet fragrance
Fruit: ¼ in across, pea-sized, persists on tree into winter

The Latin *Arbutus* and Spanish *madrone* translate to "strawberry tree," referring to the red fruits. • These trees are drought tolerant and are excellent cliff stabilizers because their long roots reach as far as the bedrock in search of water. • Medicinally, Pacific madrone was used traditionally to treat colds, stomach problems, as an astringent, as a tea to treat bladder infections, in sitz baths for other types of infections and as a postpartum contraceptive. **Where found:** canyon and mountain slopes from sea level to 5000 ft.

Pacific Dogwood

Cornus nuttallii

Height: 65 ft
Leaves: 3–4 in
Flowers: tiny, greenish-purple-tipped, in clusters surrounded by 4–6 showy, white or pinkish, 2–5 in bracts
Fruit: red berries, <½ in across, in clusters

When in flower in early spring, Pacific dogwood adds an exotic flair to the dull periphery of coniferous forests, flirting with stately pines, spruce and Douglas-fir. In fall, the leaves turn a delicate pinkish red. • This tree is becoming rare in the Pacific Northwest owing to its susceptibility to a fungal disease called anthracnose. **Where found:** moist, well-drained sites, such as along streambeds, in low-elevation mixed forests.

Oregon Ash

Fraxinus latifolia

Height: 80 ft
Leaves: compound, 5–7 leaflets, each 5 in long
Flowers: ⅛ in wide, inconspicuous
Fruit: samaras, 1¼–2 in long, in dense clusters

Oregon ash is the only native *Fraxinus* species in the Pacific Northwest. It is a member of the olive family (Oleaceae). • Deer and elk browse on this plant, and it makes good firewood. It is a popular ornamental and can be found in gardens and lining city streets. • This tree may reach 250 years of age and grows quickly in its youth, but growth slows with age. **Where found:** moist to wet soils at low elevations and near streams; north Coast Ranges and in the Sierra Nevada, prevalent in the canyons of the Pit and Sacramento rivers.

California Boxelder

Acer negundo var. *californicum*

Height: to 20–50 ft
Leaves: 2–4 in long
Flowers: inconspicuous, male and female on separate trees
Fruit: paired, V-shaped samaras, 1–1½ in long

A subspecies of *A. negundo*, which is the most widely distributed North American maple, var. *californicum* is endemic to the state and is also a popular ornamental because of its colorful and shapely fruits and leaves. It resembles an ash and is the only North American species of maple with compound leaves. • This tree grows quickly but is short-lived. Annual shoots can extend over 2 ft, but mature trees become brittle and burled and reach decadence at about 75 years of age. **Where found:** along streams or other water sources (though it is very drought resistant) in the mountains of central and northern California. **Also known as:** western boxelder, boxelder maple, maple ash.

SHRUBS

Shrubs survive several seasons and are therefore perennials. They have one or more woody stems or can be a vine, and they are normally less than 16 ft tall. Shrubs usually produce flowers and fruit. Besides providing habitat and shelter for a variety of animals, their berries, leaves and often bark are crucial sources of food for many animals. The tasty berries of some shrubs have been a staple of Native and traditional foods, and they are still enjoyed by people everywhere.

Junipers
p. 166

Prince's-pine
p. 166

Falsebox
p. 166

Heath Family
pp. 167–68

Willow
p. 169

Dogwood
pp. 169

Rose Family
pp. 169–71

Scotch Broom
p. 172

Asters
p. 172

Buckthorns
p. 173

Currants
pp. 173–74

Honeysuckles
pp. 174–75

Poison Oak
p. 175

Buckeye
p. 175

Junipers

Juniperus spp.

Height: shrubs of a few feet to tree forms of several feet
Needles: ¼–¾ in long, sometimes scale-like
Seed cones: about ½ in long

Blue-gray juniper "berries" are, in fact, tiny cones with fleshy scales. They can add spice to food and flavoring to gin, but pregnant women and people with kidney problems should never use them. They can be toxic in large quantities. • Europeans made juniper berry tea to treat eating disorders, diarrhea, and heart, lung and kidney problems. Native peoples burned branches of this pungently aromatic evergreen to purify homes, protect people from evil and bring good luck to hunters. **Where found:** dry, open sites in plains to alpine zones.

Prince's-pine

Chimaphila umbellata

Height: 4–12 in
Leaves: ¾–3 in, whorled, evergreen
Flowers: <½ in long, pink, waxy
Fruit: round capsules, ¼ in across

Prince's-pine has been used to flavor candy, soft drinks (especially root beer) and traditional beers. The leaves of this semi-woody, evergreen shrub are glossy and dark green above and pale beneath. • Native peoples used a tea made from this plant as a remedy for fluid retention, kidney or bladder problems, fevers and coughs. Several Native groups smoked the dried leaves. • These attractive plants need certain soil fungi to live, so they usually die when transplanted. They are best enjoyed in the wild. **Where found:** wooded (usually coniferous) foothills and montane zones. **Also known as:** pipsissewa.

Falsebox

Paxistima myrsinites

Height: 8–24 in
Leaves: ½–1¼ in long, leathery, shiny
Flowers: ⅛ in wide, maroon, in small clusters
Fruit: oval capsules, ⅛ in long

The glossy, stiff leaves of these low, branched, evergreen shrubs blanket the floor of many mountain forests. Sprays of falsebox are often used in flower arrangements, and overcollecting has depleted many populations. • The greenish brown to dark reddish flowers are borne in small clusters in the leaf axils. • To remember this plant's unusual scientific name, just repeat "Pa kissed ma." **Where found:** moist forests to well-drained, open sites in foothills and montane and subalpine zones. **Also known as:** mountain boxwood, *Pachistima myrsinites*.

Common Bearberry

Arctostaphylos uva-ursi

Height: 2–6 in
Leaves: ½–1¼ in long, leathery
Flowers: ⅛–¼ in long, pinkish white, urn-shaped
Fruit: berry-like drupes, ¼–½ in across, bright red

Thick, leathery evergreen leaves help this common, mat-forming shrub to survive on dry, sunny slopes where others would perish. • The "berries" are edible, but rather mealy and tasteless. Native groups cooked them and mixed them with grease or fish eggs to reduce their dryness. The glossy leaves were widely used for smoking, both alone and later with tobacco. • The long, trailing branches send down roots, and the flowers nod in small clusters. **Where found:** well-drained, open or wooded sites from foothills to alpine zones in the western portion of the state. **Also known as:** kinnikinnick.

Salal

Gaultheria shallon

Height: average 1–4 ft, up to 7 ft
Leaves: 2–4 in long, leathery, glossy
Flowers: ¼ in across, pink to white, in clusters
Fruit: bluish black berries, ¼ in across

The edible berries of salal were an important food source to Native peoples, but they are mealy and were typically dried or mixed with animal fat, fish oil or eggs. A tea made from the leaves was used to treat several ailments, and the leaves were dried along with *Arctostaphylos* leaves and smoked like tobacco. **Where found:** warm, dry, well-drained sties, tolerant of salt spray, rocky soil; from the west slope of the Cascades to the coast; conifer forests from sea level to montane zones.

Black Huckleberry

Vaccinium membranaceum

Height: 1–5 ft
Leaves: ¾–2 in long
Flowers: ¼ in long, creamy pink to yellow-pink
Fruit: blue-black berries, ¼–½ in across

Black huckleberries are among our most delicious and highly prized berries. They are plentiful in open, subalpine sites such as old burns, and in some areas, they are sold commercially. Native peoples ate them fresh, sun-dried or smoke-dried for winter use (either loose or mashed and formed into cakes). Today, huckleberries are made into jams and jellies, or used in pancakes, muffins and desserts. • The finely toothed, deciduous leaves turn red or purple in fall. **Where found:** moist, open sites in foothills and montane zones. **Also known as:** *V. globulare.*

False Azalea

Menziesia ferruginea

Height: 1½–6½ ft
Leaves: 1¼–2½ in long, in clusters along branches
Flowers: about ¼ in long, pinkish to yellowish white, urn-shaped
Fruit: oval capsules, ¼ in long

This deciduous shrub is sometimes called "fool's huckleberry," because it looks like a huckleberry, but its fruit is a dry capsule, not a berry. • Like many members of the heath family (Ericaceae), this plant contains the poison andromedotoxin. • The sticky-hairy twigs of false azalea smell skunky when crushed. The thin, dull, pale green, glandular-hairy leaves are mostly clustered near branch tips and turn crimson in fall. **Where found:** moist woods in foothills and montane zones. **Also known as:** fool's huckleberry, *M. glabella.*

Pacific Rhododendron

Rhododendron macrophyllum

Height: average 10 ft, up to 20 ft
Leaves: evergreen, 7 in long, leathery
Flowers: ¾–1½ in long, pink, bell-shaped, 15–20 in terminal clusters
Fruit: woody capsules, ¼ in long

In spring, mountainsides blush with pink blooms and the understories of coniferous forests are brightened by this colorful species. The range of this wild rhododendron is reduced where populations struggle in the wild against those who poach it for their gardens. • Rhododendrons are very poisonous plants, containing a neurotoxin called grayanotoxin. Though wild animals are wary, livestock is often careless, and this plant has to be cleared from grazing lands. **Where found:** moist to fairly dry coniferous or mixed forests; coast to mid-elevation mountains. **Also known as:** California rhododendron.

Whiteleaf Manzanita

Arctostaphylos manzanita

Height: 15 ft
Leaves: ¾–2 in long
Flowers: ¼ in long, white or pink, bell-shaped, drooping, in clusters
Fruit: berry-like drupes, ⅓–½ in across, white maturing to deep red

Manzanitas are characterized by smooth, orange or red bark and stiff, twisting branches. • An important member of the montane chaparral, this evergreen shrub is poor browsing for livestock but a valuable food source for wildlife such as coyotes, foxes and various bird species, especially grouse, which eat the fruits. • The word *manzanita* is Spanish for "little apple." **Where found:** dry slopes and canyons, chaparral, foothills, woodlands and coniferous forests; Coast Ranges and Sierra Nevada foothills; sea level to 5000 ft. **Also known as:** common manzanita.

Scouler's Willow

Salix scouleriana

Height: 6½–30 ft
Leaves: 1¼–4 in long
Catkins: ¾–1⅝ in long
Fruit: silky capsules, ¼–⅜ in long

Willows are extremely common, but it is
often difficult to identify each species. Dense, elongating flower clusters (catkins)
and buds covered by a single scale identify this group. • Scouler's willow is a spin-
dly, clumped, deciduous shrub with short, stiff, rust-colored hairs on the undersides of its leaves. The seed (female) catkins appear before the leaves and produce
long-beaked, short-stalked, hairy capsules containing tiny, silky-tufted seeds.
• Sitka willow (*S. sitchensis*) grows 3–26 ft tall, with brittle twigs, silky capsules
and catkins 2–3 in long that often appear before the leaves in spring. **Where found:**
moist to wet sites in foothills and montane zones; western in range.

Red-osier Dogwood

Cornus sericea

Height: 1½–10 ft
Leaves: ¾–4 in long, prominently veined
Flowers: <¼ in wide, white, in dense clusters
Fruit: berry-like drupes, about ¼ in wide

This attractive, hardy, deciduous shrub has
distinctive purple to red branches with white flowers in spring, red leaves in fall
and white "berries" in winter. It is easily grown from cuttings. • Native peoples
smoked the dried inner bark alone or with tobacco or common bearberry (kinnikinnick). The flexible branches were often woven into baskets, especially as
decorative red rims. The bitter, juicy berries, mixed with sweeter fruit or sugar,
made "sweet-and-sour." **Where found:** moist sites in plains, foothills and montane
zones. **Also known as:** *C. stolonifera.*

Western Mountain-ash

Sorbus scopulina

Height: 3½–13 ft
Leaves: compound, leaflets 1¼–2½ in long
Flowers: <½ in wide, white, in large, dense, flat-topped clusters
Fruit: reddish orange pomes, ¼–⅜ in across, in clusters

Deep green, glossy leaves and showy clusters of white flowers or red
"berries" make western mountain-ash an attractive deciduous shrub.
The juicy berries also provide food for many birds. Some Native peoples ate these
bitter fruits fresh or dried, but many considered them inedible. Today, they are
sometimes made into jams and jellies. **Where found:** moist sites in foothills and
montane and subalpine zones.

Thimbleberry

Rubus parviflorus

Height: 1½–6½ ft
Leaves: 2–8 in wide, 3–7-lobed, similar to a maple leaf
Flowers: 1–2 in wide, white
Fruit: raspberry-like, red, ⅝–¾ in wide

These beautiful, satiny berries are seedy and difficult to collect, but most Native peoples ate them fresh from the bush because they are so common. Thimbleberries can be tasteless, tart or sweet, depending on the season and the site, but birds and bears always seem to enjoy them. • Native peoples also ate the young shoots, and the broad, 2–8 in wide leaves provided temporary plates, containers and basket liners. • This deciduous shrub, without prickles, often forms dense thickets. **Where found:** moist to dry sites in foothills and montane zones.

Ninebark

Physocarpus capitatus

Height: 12 ft
Leaves: 1½–3½ in wide, 1⅛–2⅜ in long, 3–5-lobed
Flowers: ½ in long, white, 5 petals, in rounded clusters
Fruit: reddish brown follicles, ¼ in long, in dense, upright clusters

Althought its is slightly toxic, many Native groups used this plant medicinally, following the old adage that "what doesn't kill you, cures you." • This shrub is named for the supposedly 9 layers of bark that can be peeled away from the stem. • The leaves turn to intense reds and oranges in fall. **Where found:** low to mid elevations; wet, somewhat open places such as thickets along streams and lakes, coastal marshes and edges of moist woodlands; native to the Sierra Nevada, ranging north through Oregon and Washington.

Oceanspray

Holodiscus discolor

Height: up to 10 ft
Leaves: ¾–2½ in long, hairy
Flowers: tiny, creamy white, in dense clusters 4–7 in long
Fruit: tiny, light brown, in large clusters that persist through winter

As its name attests, this species is very tolerant of salt spray and maritime conditions, though it is also common inland on the western slopes of the Cascade Mountains. Its hardiness makes it a pioneer species on disturbed sites. • Imaginative minds have drawn comparison between the drooping clusters of tiny white flowers and frothy sea foam dripping from the shrubs hanging over coastal cliff sides. **Where found:** forest edges, cliff edges, coastline; coastal to low montane zones of the western Cascades. **Also known as:** creambush.

Shrubby Cinquefoil

Dasiphora floribunda

Height: 1–4 ft
Leaves: compound, leaflets ½–¾ in long, grayish green
Flowers: ¾ in, yellow, 5 petals
Fruit: achenes ⅝–1¼ in wide, light brown, hairy

This hardy, deciduous shrub is sometimes also seen in gardens and public places. It is often covered with bright yellow blooms from spring to fall. Shrubby cinquefoil also provides erosion control, especially along highways. • Heavily browsed cinquefoils indicate overgrazing, as most animals prefer other plants. • Native peoples used the papery, shredding bark as tinder for fires. **Where found:** wet to dry, often rocky sites from plains to subalpine zones. **Also known as:** *Potentilla fruticosa*, *Pentaphylloides floribunda*.

Bitterbrush

Purshia tridentata

Height: to 8 ft
Leaves: 1 in long
Flowers: ⅝ in long, cream-colored, tubular, solitary
Fruit: about ⅝ in long, spindle-shaped, seed-like

Bitterbrush has very similar leaves to sagebrush (though they are not aromatic), but it has small, bright yellow, rose-like flowers and velvety, seed-like fruits. It is an abundant shrub and an important member of the sagebrush community in dry parts of the state. Its hardiness and abundance makes this plant important forage for deer and elk, and the abundant yellow flowers add splashes of color to the dry landscape. **Where found:** northeastern California and dry slopes of the Sierra-Cascades. **Also known as:** antelopebrush.

Chamise

Adenostoma fasciculatum

Height: to 2–12 ft
Leaves: ¼–½ in long, sharply pointed
Flowers: small, white, 5 petals, in clusters at branch ends
Fruit: inconspicuous dry achenes

This California native is one of the most widespread and characteristic shrubs of the chaparral, forming dense stands called chamissal. Chamise is an important ground cover that prevents soil desiccation and wind erosion. • An evergreen of the rose family, the 5-petaled, white flowers turn rusty with age. • Flammable oils in the shiny leaves cause intense, dramatic wildfires, a necessary cycle to clear the dry vegetation and encourage fresh regrowth. Chamise roots and crowns survive the fire, holding the soil and soon regenerating. **Where found:** dry coastal hills and the Sierra Nevada. **Also known as:** greasewood.

171

Scotch Broom

Cytisus scoparius

Height: 6–8 ft
Leaves: ½–1 in long, divided into 3 leaflets
Flowers: ¾–1 in long, yellow
Fruit: flattened, black pods, 1–1½ in long

Bright masses of golden yellow flowers fill hedges, ditches and roadsides with radiant color, though Scotch broom is not regarded with much pleasure by botanists. This shrub is classified as a noxious weed. An invasive, introduced species from Europe, it is amazingly prolific and spreads rapidly over wide areas. Reportedly, only 3 seeds planted on Vancouver Island, Canada, in 1850, subsequently colonized the entire island. **Where found:** low elevations; open and disturbed sites; invading natural meadows and open forests.

Big Sagebrush

Artemisia tridentata

Height: 1½–6½ ft
Leaves: ½–¾ in long, silvery, 3 teeth at the tip
Flowers: very small, yellow, in heads ½–2¾ in wide
Fruit: achenes

This plant is not a true sage, but rather a species of aster. • This common shrub, with a pungent, sage-like aroma and grayish, shredding bark, has been used in a wide variety of medicines and was also burned as a smudge and fumigant. • Big sagebrush is a valuable food for many wild birds and mammals, but livestock avoid it. Early settlers knew that its presence indicated groundwater. **Where found:** often covering many acres of dry plains and slopes.

Rabbitbush

Ericameria nauseosa

Height: 8–24 in
Leaves: 1¼–2½ in long, narrow, gray-green, velvety
Flowers: ¼ in wide, yellow, in dense clusters
Fruit: tufted achenes

In late summer, this flat-topped, deciduous shrub covers dry slopes with splashes of yellow. A hardy species, this plant thrives on poor soils and in harsh conditions. • Native peoples made medicinal teas from the roots or leaves to treat coughs, colds, fevers and menstrual pain. The dense branches were used to cover and carpet sweathouses, and they were burned slowly to smoke hides. Boiled flowerheads produced a lemon yellow dye for wool, leather and baskets. **Where found:** dry, open areas on plains, foothills and in montane zones; northeastern California. **Also known as:** rubber rabbitbrush, *Chrysothamnus nauseosus*.

Deerbrush

Ceanothus integerrimus

Height: 4–8 ft
Leaves: to 2 in long, glossy
Flowers: tiny, white or blue, in plumes 2–6 in long
Fruit: dry capsules, each with a hard seed

Though this shrub has individuals with white flowers, and others have light blue or even dark blue flowers, they are all the same species of *Ceanothus*. • Deerbrush is found in association with the sagebrush community of hardy shrubs. • These shrubs are important forage for deer and other ungulates such as elk. **Where found:** Sierra and Cascade ranges.

Cascara Buckthorn

Rhamnus purshiana

Height: 16–32 ft
Leaves: 2–6 in long, oval, dark, shiny
Flowers: ⅛ in long, greenish yellow, 5 petals
Fruit: berry, ¼ in across, bright red maturing to deep purple or black

Cascara is the largest buckthorn species. • The bark was used as a natural laxative by both Native groups and settlers, and in natural medicine in modern times. The edible fruit does not have laxative properties but is not very tasty anyway. **Where found:** moist, acidic soils in shady clearings or in the understory of forest edges; mixed forests; low to mid elevations; Coast and Sierra Nevada ranges and northward. **Also known as:** Pursh's buckthorn; commercially called "cascara sagrada"; in olden times called "chitticum bark."

Bristly Black Currant

Ribes lacustre

Height: 1½–5 ft
Leaves: 1¼–1⅝ in wide, usually 5-lobed
Flowers: ¼ in wide, reddish to maroon, in clusters
Fruit: dark purple berries, ¼–⅜ in across

Many Native groups ate these edible but insipid berries, fresh or cooked. Today, bristly black currants are usually made into jam. The branch spines of this deciduous shrub cause serious allergic reactions in sensitive people, and some consider the branches (and by extension, the bristly, glandular fruit) to be poisonous.
• Wild currants are the intermediate host for blister rust, a virulent disease of native 5-needled pines. • The small flowers hang in clusters of 7–15. **Where found:** northwestern California; in moist, wooded or open sites in foothills to alpine zones.

Squaw Currant

Ribes cereum

Height: 1½–5 ft
Leaves: ¼–1 in long, ⅜–1⅝ in wide, 3–5-lobed
Flowers: <⅜ in long, white to pink, tubular, in drooping clusters
Fruit: red berries, ¼ in wide

These tasteless to bitter, berries (currants) were eaten only occasionally by Native peoples. Some considered them a tonic, whereas others ate them to relieve diarrhea. • The usually sticky-hairy, tubular flowers hang in clusters of 1–8 and are an important source of nectar for hummingbirds early in the year. • The species name *cereum* means "waxy," in reference to the waxy appearance of the glandular, often sticky-hairy leaves. **Where found:** dry sites on plains, foothills and montane slopes. **Also known as:** wax currant.

Common Snowberry

Symphoricarpos albus

Height: 1½–2½ ft
Leaves: ¾–1⅝ in long
Flowers: ⅛–¼ in long, pink to white, bell-shaped
Fruit: white, berry-like drupes, ¼–½ in across, in clusters

The name "snowberry" refers to the waxy "berries" that remain in small clusters near branch tips through winter. All parts of this deciduous shrub are toxic, causing vomiting and diarrhea. Some Native groups called the fruits "corpse berries" because they were believed to be part of the spirit world, not to be eaten by the living. **Where found:** well-drained sites from the plains to lower subalpine zones.

Twinberry

Lonicera involucrata

Height: 3½–6½ ft
Leaves: 2–6 in long
Flowers: ½–¾ in long, yellow, tubular
Fruit: black berries, <⅜ in across, in pairs

The unusual, shiny berries of these deciduous shrubs, with their broad, spreading, backward-bending, shiny red to purplish bracts, catch the eyes of passersby and also of hungry bears and birds. Despite their tempting appearance, these berries are unpalatable, and they can be toxic. **Where found:** moist to wet, usually shaded sites in foothills and montane and subalpine zones in the Sierra-Cascade ranges. **Also known as:** bracted honeysuckle.

Black Elderberry

Sambucus racemosa var. *melanocarpa*

Height: 3½–10 ft
Leaves: compound, 5–7 leaflets each 2–6 in long
Flowers: ⅛–¼ in wide, whitish, in clusters
Fruit: black, berry-like drupes, <¼ in across

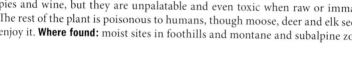

Large, showy clusters of flowers or heavy, wide "berries" draw attention to this strong-smelling, clumped, deciduous shrub. The berries can be made into jam, jelly, pies and wine, but they are unpalatable and even toxic when raw or immature. The rest of the plant is poisonous to humans, though moose, deer and elk seem to enjoy it. **Where found:** moist sites in foothills and montane and subalpine zones.

Poison Oak

Toxicodendron diversilobum

Height: 3–7 ft, sometimes vining up to 50 ft
Leaves: 3–5 irregular lobes (similar to an oak leaf), 1–2 in long
Flowers: tiny, yellow, 5 petals, in loose racemes
Fruit: berries, ¼ in across, white or cream-colored

Poison oak is not an oak, and poison ivy is not an ivy, but both are members of the sumac family (Anacardiaceae) and contain the potent allergen urushiol. This substance can stay active on unwashed clothing or on cut branches for up to a year, and smoke from burning branches can damage lung, nose and throat tissues. Not everyone is affected, but some people contract a painful, red, long-lasting rash. Avoid this plant by remembering the rhyme "Leaves of three, let it be." • The leaves turn bright scarlet in fall. **Where found:** sea level to 5000 ft.

California Buckeye

Aesculus californica

Height: 15–23 ft
Leaves: palmately compound, 5 leaflets each 2–6 in long
Flowers: 1 in long, white to pale pink, sweet-scented, in erect clusters
Fruit: pear-like, light brown, poisonous

This tall shrub is beautiful and deadly. The bark, leaves and fruit contain the neurotoxic glycoside aesculin. Even the flower nectar is lethal to honey bees, and reportedly humans have been poisoned by eating honey made from California buckeye. Native peoples ingeniously used this plant to fish with by throwing meal made from ground buckeye seeds into pools of water. The toxins in the seed meal would stupefy the fish so they would loll about on the water's surface, where they were easily caught. **Where found:** Coast, Klamath and Sierra Nevada ranges; from Siskiyou and Shasta Counties south. **Also known as:** horsechestnut.

HERBS, FERNS & SEAWEEDS

The plants in this section are all non-woody plants and include herbs, ferns and seaweeds.

Herbs and ferns can be annual, though many are perennial, growing from a persistent rootstock. Most of those with flowering stems later produce fruit. Various forms of seeds are familiar, such as those of the sunflower, a favored treat, and the dandelion, whose white parachuted seeds are irresistible fun to blow into the wind. Many of these plants can be used for adding flavor to foods, and in medicine, aromatherapy and dyes. The many different and unique flowers give us pleasure for their delicate and often breathtaking beauty in color and form. They are the inspiration of artists and poets and are often symbols of romance, or have meanings attached to them through folklore, legend or superstition.

Seaweeds are algae and can be classified into 3 major groups: green, red and brown. They absorb all the required fluids, nutrients and gases directly from the water and, unlike terrestrial plants, do not require an inner system for conducting fluids and nutrients. However, seaweeds do contain chlorophyll to absorb the sunlight needed for photosynthesis. They also contain other light-absorbing pigments, which give some seaweeds their red or brown coloration. Instead of roots, seaweeds have "holdfasts" to anchor them to the sea floor. Many seaweeds have hollow, gas-filled floats, which help to keep the photosynthetic structures of these organisms buoyant and close to the water's surface so that they can absorb sunlight. Seaweeds provide food and shelter for marine animals, and dense, underwater seaweed "forests" are an important part of many marine ecosystems. Seaweeds also provide food for humans in some cultures and have a variety of medicinal and industrial uses as well.

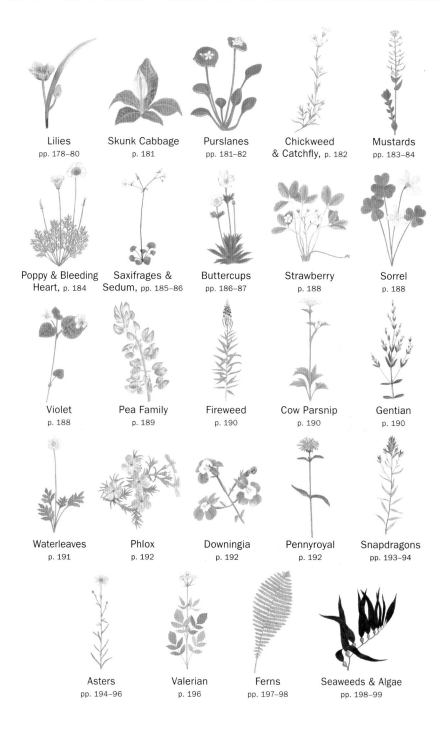

Lilies
pp. 178–80

Skunk Cabbage
p. 181

Purslanes
pp. 181–82

Chickweed
& Catchfly, p. 182

Mustards
pp. 183–84

Poppy & Bleeding
Heart, p. 184

Saxifrages &
Sedum, pp. 185–86

Buttercups
pp. 186–87

Strawberry
p. 188

Sorrel
p. 188

Violet
p. 188

Pea Family
p. 189

Fireweed
p. 190

Cow Parsnip
p. 190

Gentian
p. 190

Waterleaves
p. 191

Phlox
p. 192

Downingia
p. 192

Pennyroyal
p. 192

Snapdragons
pp. 193–94

Asters
pp. 194–96

Valerian
p. 196

Ferns
pp. 197–98

Seaweeds & Algae
pp. 198–99

Nodding Onion

Allium cernuum

Height: 4–12 in
Leaves: ⅛–¼ in wide, basal, grass-like
Flowers: ¼ in wide, pink to purplish, bell-shaped, nodding
Fruit: ⅛ in long, 3 lobed capsules (bulbs), ½–¾ in thick

When they are not in flower, wild onions are distinguished from their poisonous relative, meadow death camas, by their strong onion smell. Do not try the taste test. • Many Native groups enjoyed wild onions as a vegetable and as flavoring in other foods. Cooking decreases the strong odor and makes the bulbs sweeter and easier to digest. Bears, ground squirrels and marmots also enjoy wild onions. **Where found:** moist to dry, open sites in plains, foothills and montane zones.

Mariposa Lily

Calochortus tolmiei

Height: ½–1 in stem
Leaves: ½–1 in long, basal
Flowers: ½–1 in long, 3 petals, whitish, covered in dense, purple hairs; sepals narrow, pointed
Fruit: winged capsules, ¾–1⅛ in long

The showy flowers have distinctly different petals and sepals, unusual among lilies. • This lily gets its name *mariposa* from the Spanish word for "butterfly." The genus name *Calochortus* means "beautiful grass." • A frequently honored person in plant nomenclature is William F. Tolmie, a 19th-century Scottish naturalist and a physician with the Hudson's Bay Company. **Where found:** dry, grassy flats and slopes of the Central Valley and into northern Sacramento Valley; to 6000 ft. **Also known as:** Tolmie's ears, pussy ears.

Corn Lily

Clintonia uniflora

Height: 2½–6 in
Leaves: 3–6 in long, 1¼–2 in wide, basal
Flowers: ¾–1 in wide, solitary
Fruit: single berry, ⅜–½ in wide

This common woodland wildflower brightens the forest floor in spring and early summer. The 2–4 slightly fleshy, glossy basal leaves have hairy edges. • Although the bright metallic blue berries are unpalatable by human standards, grouse seem to enjoy them. • This native perennial can live for 30 or more years. **Where found:** moist to wet, montane and subalpine forests and clearings. **Also known as:** clintonia, bride's bonnet, queen's cup.

Chocolate Lily

Fritillaria lanceolata

Height: 30 in
Leaves: 2–6 in long, 1–2 whorls of 3–5
Flowers: nodding bells, 1½ in long, single or in clusters of 2–5
Fruit: upright, 6-angled capsules with wings

The bulbs of this lily are edible and were eaten by coastal Native groups. They boiled the bulbs as well as the "bulblets," which are said to be similar to rice, though bitter. • Today, this flower is very rare and should be left undisturbed—and uneaten. **Where found:** grassy meadows, open woods; sea level to nearly subalpine; along the coast and inland along major drainages. **Also known as:** checker lily, mission bells, *F. affinis.*

False Lily-of-the-Valley

Maianthemum dilatatum

Height: 4–15¾ in
Leaves: 1–3, alternate, heart-shaped, up to 4 in long
Flowers: tiny, with parts in 4s, in terminal cylindrical clusters
Fruit: round berries, ¼ in across, light green to brown, maturing to red

Inspiring myths throughout recorded time, the flowers of this plant supposedly grew from the tears of the Virgin and the blood of saints in Christianity. They were also regarded as sacred to the goddess Maia and the god Hermes and thus were significant in alchemy and astrology. • In Haida myth, the berries were part of a feast for supernatural beings. **Where found:** moist to wet, usually shady woods and riverside areas; low to mid elevations. **Also known as:** maianthemum, deerberry, snakeberry, mayflower, may lily, two-leaved Solomon's-seal, wild lily-of-the-valley.

Star-flowered False Solomon's-seal

Maianthemum stellatum

Height: ½–2 ft
Leaves: 1¼–4¾ in long
Flowers: <½ in wide, white
Fruit: berries, ¼–½ in across

The species name *stellata*, from the Latin *stella*, "star," aptly describes the radiant, white blossoms of this woodland wildflower. • This unbranched, slightly arching plant produces clusters of dark blue or reddish black berries, which are greenish yellow with purplish stripes when young. **Where found:** moist to dry sites in foothills to subalpine zones. **Also known as:** *Smilacina stellata.*

Western Trillium

Trillium ovatum

Height: 4–16 in
Leaves: 2–6 in long, in whorls of 3
Flowers: 2½–3½ in across, white
Fruit: berry-like capsules, green, slightly winged

This wildflower is one of the first showy blooms to grace the forest each spring. • Trillium, from the Latin *tri*, "three," refers to the 3 leaves, 3 petals, 3 sepals and 3 stigmas. • Each seed has a small, oil-rich body that attracts ants. The ants carry seeds to their nests, eat the oil-rich part and discard the rest, thus dispersing and planting new trilliums. • The fruits are numerous yellowish green, berry-like capsules, which are shed in a sticky mass. **Where found:** moist to wet, shady sites from foothills to subalpine zones.

California False-Hellebore

Veratrum californicum

Height: 3–5 ft
Leaves: 6–16 in long, 2–6 in wide
Flowers: 1 in wide, white to greenish, star-like, in terminal clusters
Fruit: egg-shaped capsules, ¾–1⅛ in long

Alternating, corn-like leaves give this plant one of its common names, corn lily, but it is by no means edible. False-hellebores are members of a very poisonous group of plants. A similar species, green false-hellebore (*V. viride*) is one of the most poisonous plants in the Pacific Northwest. Livestock are often not wary, and eating this plant causes severe deformities in their offspring, particularly in sheep. **Where found:** wet areas throughout the Sierras. **Also known as:** corn lily.

Meadow Death Camas

Zigadenus venenosus

Height: 18–23 in
Leaves: up to 12 in long
Flowers: tiny, white, saucer-shaped, in a terminal cluster 6–8 in long
Fruit: 3-lobed capsules, ¾ in long

Deadly poisonous, the bulbs of this plant are very similar in appearance to those of the blue-flowered edible camas (*Camassia* spp.), or quamash, which was an important food staple to Native groups and often grows alongside death camas. The edible variety is easily identifiable by the flowers (purple vs. white). • This plant is notorious for poisoning sheep and occasionally other livestock, but well-fed animals usually avoid it. Ingestion results in convulsions, coma, and then death. **Where found:** wet areas, open forests or forest edges, rocky or grassy slopes; low to mid elevations.

Skunk Cabbage

Lysichiton americanum

Height: 1–5 ft
Leaves: 40–60 in long, 20 in wide, in a large, basal rosette
Flowers: tiny, greenish yellow, in a spike up to 14 in tall
Fruit: berry-like, pulpy, green-yellow

Skunk cabbage belongs to the large and worldwide arum family (Araceae). • The complex inflorescence consists of an encircling yellow spathe and a central columnar spadix packed with hundreds of tiny, yellowish flowers. The flower emits a strong, skunky scent that attracts small beetles to pollinate it. • Native peoples used the large leaves for packaging, lining berry baskets and serving food, lending it the nickname "Indian wax paper." • Grizzly bears eat skunk cabbage, so hikers beware. **Where found:** moist or wet sites, marshes, bogs, swamps; low and mid elevations; near coastal conifer forests.

Western Springbeauty

Claytonia lanceolata

Height: 2–4 in
Leaves: ⅝–2½ in long, stem leaves opposite
Flowers: ½–⅝ in wide, white or pale pink
Fruit: egg-shaped capsules, ⅛ in long

These delicate, fleshy perennials are often found hugging the ground near late snow patches at high elevations. • The leaves are edible, and the corms are said to taste like mild radishes when raw and like potatoes when cooked. Native peoples collected the deep-growing, small, wide corms in spring, as the white to pinkish blossoms faded. **Where found:** moist, open sites in foothills to alpine zones.

Miner's Lettuce

Claytonia perfoliata

Height: 1–16 in
Leaves: up to 4 in wide, 2 stem leaves usually fused into a disk
Flowers: ⅛–¼ in wide, numerous (5–40), white or pinkish
Fruit: 3-segmented capsules

Remarkably fleshy, succulent leaves make this species easily distinguishable. These juicy basal leaves completely encircle the stem to showcase the tiny, delicate flowers. • The common name comes from the fact that early settlers (and miners) collected this plant for salads. The genus name *Claytonia* honors John Clayton, an early botanist of note. **Where found:** moist open to shady sites, often sandy soils; forests, thickets, meadows, disturbed sites; low to mid elevations (below 6000 ft). **Also known as:** *Montia perfoliata*.

Threeleaf Lewisia

Lewisia triphylla

Height: 1–4 in
Leaves: ⅜–2 in long, 2–3 paired or whorled
Flowers: ½ in wide, white or pinkish with darker veins
Fruit: capsules, ⅛ in long

Named *triphylla* for its 3 leaves, this plant most often only displays 2. There are no basal leaves, and the 2 upper, fleshy leaves are opposite each other and upward-pointing like a set of wings. The flowers have 5–9 petals and 3–5 stamens with colorful anthers. • This is a favored plant for rock gardens and is sometimes overcollected from the wild. • The genus *Lewisia* is named in honor of Captain Meriwether Lewis of the Lewis and Clark expeditions. **Where found:** moist, sandy sites, damp areas or on bare ground; Cascade and Coast ranges; 5000–11,000 ft.

Field Chickweed

Cerastium arvense

Height: 2–12 in
Leaves: ½–1¼ in long, narrow
Flowers: ⅛–½ in wide, white, in open, flat-topped clusters
Fruit: capsules, 2–3½ in long

Aptly named, chickweed was fed to chickens, goslings and caged birds, especially when the birds were ill. • The genus name *Cerastium* comes from the Greek *kerastes*, "horned," in reference to the curved, cylindrical capsules, which open by 10 small teeth at the tip. The leaves of this loosely clumped perennial often have secondary, leafy tufts in their axils. **Where found:** dry, open, often rocky sites in plains to alpine zones.

Seabluff Catchfly

Silene douglasii

Height: 4–16 in
Leaves: ¾ to 3 in long, hairy
Flowers: petals ½ in long, white to greenish or pinkish, sepals ½ in long, fused in a chalice
Fruit: capsule, ⅜–½ in long

The long, slender stem of seabluff catchfly is covered with tiny hairs and bears either a terminal flower or branches off into several stalks, each with a flower head. Usually several plants will grow in a clump, resembling erect bouquets of flowers above low, lush, green leaves. **Where found:** dry flats, gravelly sites, forest openings; throughout the Sierras at 5000–9000 ft to the coastal ranges of Northern California and to the Cascades. **Also known as:** Douglas' catchfly.

American Winter Cress

Barbarea orthoceras

Height: ½–2 ft
Leaves: to 4½ in long, becoming simpler and smaller higher up the stem
Flowers: ½ in long, yellow, 4-petaled, clustered in a raceme
Fruit: seedpods (siliques), to 2 in long

This biennial herb grows fairly tall and erect from its woody base and explodes in bright yellow flower clusters. The leaves are interesting and distinctive, with 2–3 pairs of smaller lobes and one large lobe. **Where found:** moist to wet forests and openings; meadows, streambanks, beaches; low to mid elevations.

Field Mustard

Brassica rapa

Height: 1–6 ft
Leaves: up to 12 in long, lobed, becoming simpler and smaller higher up the stem
Flowers: yellow, 4 petals, ½ in wide
Fruit: narrow pods, 1–2 in long

Golden fields of mustard in spring are a beautiful sight and often one of the first splashes of color to announce spring. • Though there are many genera in the mustard family, the *Brassica* are the ones that most commonly come to mind. A member of a group of cultivated plants, *Brassica* is Latin for "cabbage," and *rapa* means "turnip." The word "mustard" appears to derive from the Latin *mustum* for "new wine," which was the first pressing of the grapes and was mixed with crushed mustard seeds to make a sauce. **Where found:** agricultural areas below 4000 ft. **Also known as:** rapeseed, *B. campestris*.

Milk Maids

Cardamine californica

Height: 1½–2 ft
Leaves: ½–2¾ in long, rounded
Flowers: ½–¾ in wide, 4 petals
Fruit: seedpods, up to 2 in long

One of the first plants to flower in spring, this plant's pale pink or white flowers are commonly seen in shady canyons, on foothill slopes, in woodlands and in shady gardens, often early in the new year. In wet areas, they can grow in exuberant masses. **Where found:** shady canyons and woodlands below 3500 ft. **Also known as:** toothwort, *Dentaria californica*.

Peppergrass

Lepidium nitidum

Height: 4–16 in
Leaves: alternate, becoming smaller higher up the stem
Flowers: ¼ in across
Fruit: oval seedpod, ¼ in long

Many mustards are more noticeable for their seedpods than for their flowers, and peppergrass is no exception. When the tiny, white flowers go to seed, they drop their petals, and the seedpods mature from green to a gorgeous reddish purple. The seedpods give this species its common name because they are shiny and peppery-tasting. **Where found:** in large patches on dry flats, grassy slopes and disturbed sites below 3000 ft.

California Poppy

Eschscholtzia californica

Height: 2–24 in
Leaves: mostly basal, highly divided (parsley-like)
Flowers: solitary, yellow to orange, 4 petals, to 2 in wide
Fruit: pod-like capsules

The state flower of California, this bright and showy species sets fields and slopes ablaze with orange and gold. There are many varieties of California poppy, but the flowers all have a distinctive pink pedestal, like a platter, with the bloom showcased atop. This plant is more noticeable once the leaves fall and only the fat, dry seedpods remain. **Where found:** roadsides, clearings, dry rocky slopes; low elevations.

Pacific Bleeding Heart

Dicentra formosa

Height: 6–20 in
Leaves: 12 in long, basal, fern-like
Flowers: pink-purple, heart-shaped, ¾–1 in long
Fruit: small, oblong capsules

Native to North America and Asia, the common name refers to the heart-shaped flower, which ranges in color from light pink to intense deep purple or magenta. This plant is also cultivated and highly hybridized in color and size for gardens. The soft leafy fern-like foliage is one of the common lush, green groundcovers in shady, moist forests. **Where found:** moist sites along ravines and streambanks and in forests; low to mid elevations. **Also known as:** western bleeding heart.

Small-flowered Woodland Star

Lithophragma parviflorum

Height: 1–3 ft
Leaves: 1–2 in, 3-lobed, basal
Flowers: ½ in across, white to pink, 4–14 alternately arranged up the stem
Fruit: 3-chambered capsules

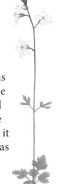

Caught up in a breeze, these star-like flowers atop their slender stems sway like magic wands conducting spells across the meadows. The white, pink or lavender flowers have 5 petals, each with 3 lobes, and are closely attached to the stems. • This flower makes its appearance in spring on wooded foothills where, typical of the saxifrage family, it finds its preferred rocky habitat. **Where found:** grassy slopes, open areas with rocky soil, dry forests, coastal bluffs; low to mid elevations.

Fringed Grass-of-Parnassus

Parnassia fimbriata

Height: 4–12 in
Leaves: ¾–1⅝ in wide, mostly basal, glossy
Flowers: ¾ in wide, white, solitary
Fruit: capsules, <½ in long

The 5 distinctively fringed, pale-veined petals of these delicate flowers are unmistakable—hence the name *fimbriata*, which means "fringed." Each flower has 5 fertile stamens and 5 sterile stamens tipped with 5–9 glands. The genus name *Parnassia* comes from Parnassus, a Greek island sacred to Apollo and the Muses. • Northern grass-of-Parnassus (*P. palustris*) is similar and widespread, but has smooth-edged petals and large, sterile stamens tipped with 7–15 glands. **Where found:** wet sites in montane, subalpine and alpine zones.

Brook Saxifrage

Saxifraga odontoloma

Height: ½–1½ ft
Leaves: up to 8 in long, basal, toothed
Flowers: ¼ in across, 5 petals
Fruit: capsules, ¼ in long

Saxifrage means "stone breaker," referring the preference of some species for rocky habitats such as mountain ridges or even stone walls. • Brook saxifrage displays all the characteristics of a typical saxifrage: a leafless stem rising above large, round, basal, scallop-toothed leaves and many gracefully hanging flowers with spade-shaped white petals and contrasting yellow dots. **Where found:** wet meadows and along mountain streams in mid to high elevations of the Sierras.

Pacific Sedum

Sedum spathulifolium

Height: 2–12 in
Leaves: ¾ in long, ⅜ in wide, basal
Flowers: ⅜ in long, yellow, in flat-topped clusters
Fruit: erect follicles in 5 segments

Stonecrops are noted for their distinctive succulent leaves, a strategy to conserve water in dry habitats. Pacific sedum has crowded, succulent, wedge-shaped leaves that alternate to form a basal rosette. These delicate leaves turn reddish if exposed to full sunshine; however, they remain green long after being picked, giving them the colloquial name of "livelong." **Where found:** shady to partially shady rocky sites or coarse soils, mountain cliffs, coastal bluffs, forest openings; low to mid elevations. **Also known as:** broad-leaved stonecrop.

Windflower

Anemone drummondii

Height: 4–10 in
Leaves: ¾–2 in long
Flowers: 1–1½ in wide
Fruit: achenes, <1 inch long, in clusters

A burst of yellow stamens and 5–8 white or bluish sepals are the showy parts of this flower, which doesn't actually have true petals. After the flowers fade, the woolly, spherical fruits catch our interest, looking like wind-tousled heads and giving the plant its common name as well as the genus name *Anemone*, which means "shaken in the wind." • This plant thrives in windy, high-alpine conditions. **Where found:** rocky areas in mid to high elevations. **Also known as:** Drummond's anemone, alpine anemone.

Western Columbine

Aquilegia formosa

Height: 1–4 ft
Leaves: variable, usually twice divided into 3s, ⅜–2 in long
Flowers: 1–1½ in long, tubular, red and yellow with reddish spurs
Fruit: 5 erect follicles with hairy, spreading tips

This plant's colorful flowers entice hummingbirds, butterflies and people to sip their sweet nectar, though the latter do a poor job at pollinating. The entire flower is edible and decorative in salads. **Where found:** moist, open to partly shady meadows, forest openings, clearings, rocky slopes, beaches; low elevation to treeline. **Also known as:** crimson columbine, red columbine.

Marsh Marigold

Caltha leptosepala

Height: 4–12 in
Leaves: to 2½ in long, 1–3 in wide, basal
Flowers: ¾–1½ in wide, white or greenish
Fruit: up to ¾ in long, beaked, bright yellow-green

This species has a few distinctive, eye-catching characteristics that help to identify it. Marsh marigold has large, fleshy basal leaves, 5–10 or more showy, white sepals and many bright yellow-green stamens and pistils clumped in the center of the flower. • Native groups in Alaska enjoyed eating many parts of this species, yet for some reason, the plant was not so appreciated in our area. **Where found:** marshy sites in meadows or along streambanks, throughout the Sierra from 4000–10,500 ft. **Also known as:** alpine white marsh marigold.

Western Buttercup

Ranunculus occidentalis

Height: ½–2 ft
Leaves: variable, 1–4 in long
Flowers: ½–1 in wide, yellow
Fruit: spherical head of 5–20 tiny achenes

The butter analogy only goes as far as the color, not to any culinary uses—this plant is poisonous to people and livestock. However, buttercup essence is popular and is derived for use in holistic treatments. It is said to help the soul realize its inner light and beauty. **Where found:** damp meadows, grassy slopes, coastal bluffs, sagebrush scrub and forest openings; Sierra Nevada, 300–7000 ft.

Meadowrue

Thalictrum spp.

Height: 1–5 ft
Leaves: ½–2 in long, divided 3–4 times into 3s
Flowers: sepals <1 inch, petals absent
Fruit: achenes, <1 inch long

These tall, delicate woodland plants produce inconspicuous, greenish to purplish, male or female flowers without petals. The flowers have long sepals and either dangling anthers or greenish to purplish, lance-shaped fruits (achenes) in loose clusters, depending on the time of year. • The pleasant-smelling plants and seeds were burned in smudges or stored with possessions as insect repellent and perfume. Chewed seeds were rubbed onto hair and skin as perfume. **Where found:** moist sites in foothills, and montane and subalpine zones.

Beach Strawberry

Fragaria chiloensis

Height: to 10 in
Leaves: to 8 in, leathery, 3 leaflets
Flowers: to 1½ in wide, 5–7 petals
Fruit: strawberry, to ½ in wide

There are several species of strawberry in various habitats in our area, always distinguishable by the spreading runners, white flowers and, of course, sweet red fruits. This species, however, is one of the parents of all cultivated strawberries (*F. virginiana* is another and looks very similar). • The fruits of beach strawberry can be made into jams, pies and other sweet treats, but they are tiny and take some patience to collect in quantity and self-control to not simply pop them into one's mouth! **Where found:** sand dunes, sea bluffs, beaches; sea level. **Also known as:** coastal strawberry.

Redwood Sorrel

Oxalis oregana

Height: 2–6 in
Leaves: 2–8 in long, basal, long-stalked
Flowers: ½–¾ in long, white to pinkish with reddish veins, 5 petals
Fruit: 5-chambered capsule, ¼–⅜ in long

The 3 heart-shaped leaflets of redwood sorrel leaves could be mistaken for those of clover. Sorrel leaves fold downward at night, in direct sunlight or in the rain but otherwise are held out horizontally. • This sour-tasting plant produces oxalic acid. Native groups did eat sorrel leaves, but they can be toxic in large quantities. **Where found:** moist sites, meadows and open forests; low to mid elevations.

Wood Violet

Viola glabella

Height: to 20 in
Leaves: to 2 in wide, heart-shaped
Flowers: ⅝ in long, yellow
Fruit: capsules

Though this species is yellow, violets can be various colors, from the typical violet-blue to white to yellow, often with violet-colored stripes on the lower 3 petals. • Wood violet is very hardy, resistant to most diseases and also very prolific. A successful pioneer species in clearings and disturbed sites, it produces numerous brown seeds in explosive capsules and can populate available ground space quickly. **Where found:** moist forests, glades, clearings, streamsides; all elevations. **Also known as:** pioneer violet, yellow wood violet.

Broadleaf Lupine

Lupinus polyphyllus

Height: to 5 ft
Leaves: to 5 in long, with 10–17 leaflets
Flowers: ½ in long, in dense clusters 3–16 in long
Fruit: seedpods, to 2 in long

These attractive perennials, with their showy flower clusters and fuzzy seedpods, enrich the soil with nitrogen. • The pods look like hairy garden peas, and children may incorrectly assume that they are edible. Many lupines contain poisonous alkaloids, and it is difficult to distinguish between poisonous and non-poisonous species. • The leaves are silvery-hairy, and the pea-like flowers have silky upper sides. **Where found:** wet, open areas and disturbed sites; low to mid elevations.

Clovers

Trifolium spp.

Height: from 1–10 in depending on the species
Leaves: divided into 3 leaflets, variable in size depending on the species
Flowers: tiny, in dense flower heads
Fruit: pods, variable in size depending on the species

Clovers are some of the most familiar flowering plants, beloved for their promise of luck to those who find a "leaf of four." Although clovers are quickly identifiable, they can be quite diverse in color, ranging from white to bright fuchsia, and in size, varying from tiny species that hide in the grass to tall, proud species with lofty leaves. • The flower heads are actually a tight cluster of small flowers. **Where found:** various grassy habitats; low to subalpine elevations; often invasive.

Winter Vetch

Vicia villosa

Height: vine, 2–5 ft long
Leaves: hairy, divided into 5–10 pairs of narrow leaflets, each 1–2 in long, leaf tips with tendrils
Flowers: ¾ in long, in a long-stalked cluster of 10–40 flowers
Fruit: smooth pods, ½–¾ in long

An introduced annual or biennial, this vetch thrives in our climate. It is very hairy overall with often 2-toned flowers that combine reds or purples with white. East of the Cascades, its abundance is visible, with entire hillsides often tinted purple with these flowers. • Vetch flowers are longer than wide, differentiating them from lupine, wild pea and lotus flowers. **Where found:** disturbed sites, roadsides, fields; below 3000 ft; Sacramento area. **Also known as:** woolly vetch.

189

Fireweed

Epilobium angustifolium

Height: 1–10 ft
Leaves: ¾–8 in, lance-shaped
Flowers: ¾–1⅝ in wide, in long, erect clusters
Fruit: narrow, pod-like capsules, 1⅝–3 in long

Fireweed helps heal landscape scars (e.g., roadsides, burned forests) by blanketing the ground with colonies of plants, often producing a sea of deep pink flowers. • Young shoots can be eaten like asparagus, and the flowers can be added to salads. • The erect pods split lengthwise to release hundreds of tiny seeds tipped with fluffy, white hairs. **Where found:** open, often disturbed sites in foothills to subalpine zones.

Cow Parsnip

Heracleum lanatum

Height: up to 10 ft
Leaves: 6–16 in long, divided into 3 large segments
Flowers: tiny, white, in large, flat-topped clusters up to 1 ft wide
Fruit: ¼–½ in long

The tiny flowers are in contrast to the overall largeness of this member of the carrot family (Apiaceae). Even its genus name derives from the great Hercules of Greek mythology. • Cow parsnip can cause skin irritation because it contains phototoxic furanocoumarins that are activated by exposure to sunlight. The plant is edible and was a valuable staple to many Native groups. Be careful not to confuse it with highly poisonous hemlock species that are similar in appearance. **Where found:** streambanks, moist slopes and clearings, upper beaches, marshes; sea level to subalpine elevations. **Also known as:** *H. sphondylium.*

Northern Gentian

Gentianella amarella

Height: 4–20 in
Leaves: 2 in long, in pairs
Flowers: <1 in long, bluish. tubular
Fruit: capsules

The flowers, about the width of a dime, have petals that range in color from blue to pink-violet to purple and that barely extend past the green sepals. The basal leaves are egg-shaped, form a cluster and fade early in the season, while the pairs of narrower stem leaves persist. • The genus name *Gentianella* means "little gentian," having been split off from the genus *Gentiana*. **Where found:** moist meadows and clearings, 5000–11,000 ft; east of the Sierras; also Klamath Ranges, High Cascade Range, High Sierra Nevada, San Bernardino Mountains, White and Inyo mountains. **Also known as:** felwort.

Western Waterleaf

Hydrophyllum occidentale

Height: ½–2 ft
Leaves: divided into 7–15 segments, each 1½ in long
Flowers: tiny, lavender, bell-shaped, in clusters
Fruit: ovoid capsules, about ⅛–¼ in wide with 1–3 seeds

The somewhat hairy, somewhat cupped leaves of this plant are adapted to collect and hold a bit of water, hence their namesake. • The dense inflorescence has a hairy appearance owing to the long stamens and pistils that reach out of the flowers by about a ½ inch. **Where found:** moist woods, forest openings; foothills to mid-mountain elevations; throughout the Sierra Nevada from 2500–9500 ft, extending to the Oregon Cascades. **Also known as:** California waterleaf.

Baby Blue-eyes

Nemophila menziesii

Height: 4–12 in
Leaves: 1–2 in long, deeply 5–13-lobed
Flowers: 1½ in across, bowl-shaped, blue with white center
Fruit: capsules, ¼–½ in wide

When scattered among the green grass of the foothills in spring, baby blue-eyes wink and capture your own eyes with their beauty. • The species name for this lovely flower honors 18th-century naturalist and explorer Archibald Menzies. **Where found:** grassy flats, meadows, forest openings and slopes on the Central Coast and in the southern Coast ranges; east of the Sierra Nevada; 50–5000 ft.

Varileaf Phacelia

Phacelia heterophylla

Height: up to 4 ft
Leaves: varying lengths diminishing up the stem
Flowers: ¼ in wide, white to greenish
Fruit: ovoid capsule, ⅛ in long

In spring, this entire plant has an overall fuzzy, green appearance, with the numerous flower heads appearing as tight green spheres. The flowers, which have long, protruding stamens, bloom in tight clusters that form an inflorescence reminiscent of either fuzzy caterpillar or a coiled scorpion tail. The flower eventually fades to a rusty color, and the plant becomes inconspicuous. • The leaves of this plant vary in size and shape, giving it both its common name and the species name *heterophylla*, which is Greek for "varied leaf." **Where found:** dry areas on slopes and flats throughout the Sierras; mid to high elevations; extends to the Oregon Cascades.

Spreading Phlox

Phlox diffusa

Height: 2–4 in
Leaves: ¼–¾ in long, paired
Flowers: ½–¾ in wide, white, pink or bluish, solitary
Fruit: 3-chambered capsule

This phlox gets its name for its beautiful way of pouring over rocks in low, loose mats that carpet the ground with dense greenery or, when in bloom, blankets of brightly colored flowers. Each sweet-smelling blossom is a pinwheel-like fan of 5 petals fused at their bases into a tube ⅜–⅝ in long. **Where found:** open, rocky outcrops, slopes and scree, open forests; low montane to above treeline.

Toothed Downingia

Downingia cuspidata

Height: 2–6 in
Leaves: ¼–½ in long, narrow
Flowers: ¼–½ in long, blue to lavender with a white center and a yellow spot
Fruit: capsule, 1¼–2¾ in long

This member of the bluebell family (Campanulaceae) usually has bright blue flowers, but also occurs with very pale lavender or almost white variations. However, the blossoms always have a large, yellow spot, which can be slightly divided into 2 spots, at the base of the lower corolla lip. The top 2 petals are very narrow and stick up like rabbit's ears. **Where found:** dried mud bottoms of vernal pools, wet meadows; below 1600 ft; San Joaquin Valley and foothills of Sierra and Coast ranges.

Pennyroyal

Monardella odoratissima

Height: 1½–2 ft
Leaves: ¼–1¾ in long, in pairs
Flowers: ⅜–½ in long, whitish to pale purple or pink, in terminal clusters
Fruit: oblong nutlets

This plant's strong scent will leave no doubt that it is a mint, and its flavor is so strong that even cold water will become infused. In addition, the square stem is a telltale characteristic of members of the mint family (Lamiaceae). • The flower heads are composed of many small flowers with long bracts and protruding stamens, and these plants typically grow in crowded masses, filling areas with color and fragrance. **Where found:** dry slopes and sagebrush scrub, montane forests; Sierra and Coast ranges, Klamath ranges, High North Coast ranges, High Cascade Range, High Sierra Nevada, Modoc Plateau, White and Inyo mountains. **Also known as:** mountain monardella, coyote mint.

Scarlet Paintbrush

Castilleja miniata

Height: 8–24 in
Leaves: 2–2¾ in long
Flowers: ¾ –1¼ in long, greenish, tubular, concealed by hairy, red bracts
Fruit: 2-celled capsules

It is usually easy to recognize a paintbrush, but *Castilleja* is a confusing genus, with many flower shapes and colors and species that often hybridize. • Paintbrushes have reduced photosynthetic abilities and partially parasitize nearby plants to steal nutrients.
• Showy, leaf-like bracts give these flower clusters their red color. The actual flowers are the tubular, greenish blossoms concealed within the bracts. **Where found:** open woods and meadows, grassy slopes, tidal marshes, disturbed sites; foothills and montane zones. **Also known as:** common red paintbrush, giant paintbrush, great red paintbrush.

Yellow Monkeyflower

Mimulus guttatus

Height: 4–20 in
Leaves: ½–2 in long, in pairs
Flowers: ½–1⅝ in long, yellow, trumpet-shaped
Fruit: oblong capsules, ½–¾ in long

These snapdragons brighten streamsides, rocky seeps and wet ditches. • *Mimulus* is the diminutive form of the Latin *mimus,* meaning "a buffoon or actor in a farce or mime." The common name also alludes to the fancied resemblance of these flowers to small, grinning, ape-like faces. • This variable species often roots from nodes or sends out stolons. **Where found:** wet sites in foothills and montane and subalpine zones. **Also known as:** seep monkeyflower.

Davidson's Penstemon

Penstemon davidsonii

Height: 4–6 in
Leaves: ¼–⅝ in, mat-forming
Flowers: 1–2 in long, tubular
Fruit: narrowly winged capsules, ⅓ in long

The richly purple to lavender blue flowers are relatively large compared to the small evergreen leaves and low growth form of this plant. The 5 petals unite into long, 2-lipped tubes that stand out like loud purple trumpets among the drab-colored rocks that are this plant's preferred habitat. The throats and anthers of the flowers are woolly, adding to the interest of these showy flowers. **Where found:** rocky ridges near and above treeline throughout the Sierra Nevada and extending to the Cascades. **Also known as:** alpine penstemon.

American Brooklime

Veronica americana

Height: 4–27½ in
Leaves: to 2 in long
Flowers: ¼ in wide, saucer-shaped
Fruit: round capsules, ⅛ in long

The leaves of American brooklime are edible and commonly used in salads or as a potherb. Because this plant most often grows directly in water, be sure not to collect the leaves from plants in polluted sites. • The showy flowers are blue to violet, sometimes white, with red-purple markings and 2 large, reaching stamens that look like antennae. **Where found:** shallow water alongside slow-moving streams, springs, marshes, seepage areas, wet meadows, clearings and ditches; low to mid elevations. **Also known as:** American speedwell.

Common Yarrow

Achillea millefolium

Height: 4–31 in
Leaves: 1¼–4 in long, fern-like
Flowers: <¼ in wide, white or pinkish with cream-colored centers,
in clusters
Fruit: hairless, flattened achenes

This hardy, aromatic perennial has served for thousands of years as a fumigant, insecticide and medicine. The Greek hero Achilles, for whom the genus was named, supposedly used it to heal his soldiers' wounds after battle. • Yarrow is also an attractive ornamental, but beware—its extensive underground stems (rhizomes) can soon invade your garden. **Where found:** dry to moist, open sites from plains to alpine zones.

Leafy Aster

Symphyotrichum foliaceum var. *foliaceum*

Height: ½–3 ft
Leaves: 2–6 in long
Flowers: ray flowers ⅓–¾ in long; disk flowers tiny, yellow
Fruit: hairy achenes

One of the loveliest flowers in our area is also one of the most common. The yellow disk flowers in the center of the inflorescence are surrounded by ray flowers that can range in color from white to blue to pink, purple or red. Directly below the inflorescence is a collar of many green, leafy bracts that stick out perpendicular to the stem. **Where found:** open woods, meadows, streambanks; throughout the Sierras; mid to high elevations (5000–8000 ft). **Also known as:** leafy-headed aster, *Aster foliaceus*.

Brass Buttons

Cotula coronopifolia

Height: 8–16 in
Leaves: ⅜–1⅜ in long, narrow
Flowers: ¼–½ in wide, yellow, rays absent
Fruit: achenes

True to their name, the showy, bright yellow, disk-shaped
flower heads of this plant look like shiny brass buttons, and they
are also pleasantly aromatic. • Brass buttons is a South African
species introduced to our area, as well as to many other parts of the
world, where it typically colonizes beaches. It is very salt tolerant but also brightens up brackish, muddy, non-coastal sites. **Where found:** beaches, tidal mudflats, marshes, salt marshes, estuaries; along the coast and near inland vernal pools. **Also known as:** mud disk, golden buttons, buttonweed.

Subalpine Fleabane

Erigeron peregrinus

Height: 4–28 in
Leaves: ½–8 in long
Flowers: ray flowers 30–80, pink or purplish; disk flowers
   yellow; in heads ¾–2½ in wide
Fruit: hairy, ribbed achenes with hair-like parachutes

Fleabanes, a type of daisy, are easily confused with
asters. Aster flower heads usually have overlapping rows of
bracts with light, parchment-like bases and green tips. Fleabanes usually have 1
row of slender bracts with the same texture and color (not green) throughout.
Also, fleabanes generally flower earlier and have narrower, more numerous rays.
Where found: moist to wet, open sites in foothills to alpine zones. **Also known as:**
subalpine daisy.

Common Tarweed

Madia elegans

Height: 1–3 ft
Leaves: ¾–8 in long
Flowers: ray flowers ⅜–⅝ in long, yellow; disk flowers yellow;
   in heads 1–1½ in wide
Fruit: achenes

The long, golden, petal-like ray flowers are often 2-toned, with
either white or dark red to maroon at the base. • The name "tarweed" refers to the plant's sticky, black, glandular hairs, which readily adhere to
skin and clothing upon contact. The fragrance of tarweed is also heavy and sticky,
almost tar-like. **Where found:** grassy fields below 3000 ft. **Also known as:** common
madia, elegant tarweed.

Woolly Mule Ears

Wyethia mollis

Height: 10–20 in
Leaves: 8–16 in long, gray-green, mostly basal
Flowers: ray flowers 5–20, yellow; disk flowers yellow; in heads up to 4 in wide
Fruit: achenes, ⅜ in long

Large masses of woolly mule ears often cover mid-elevation meadows, indicating that the hillside they are growing on is almost definitely of volcanic origin. The long roots of this species can reach deep into the porous volcanic soil to find water that other plants cannot access. • The name "mule ears" refers to this plant's relatively large leaves, which grow vertically upward. The plant's dense woolly hairs and leaf growth formation help reduce water loss. **Where found:** open slopes at 4000–10,500 ft in the Sierras to southeastern Oregon. **Also known as:** narrow-leaved mule ears.

Heart-leaved Arnica

Arnica cordifolia

Height: 4–24 in
Leaves: 1⅝–4 in, basal, long-stemmed
Flowers: in heads 1–2½ in wide
Fruit: achene, ¼–⅜ in long

Some Native groups used these yellow wildflowers in love charms because of their heart-shaped leaves. The rootstocks and flowers were used in washes and poultices for treating bruises, sprains and swollen feet, but these poisonous plants should never be applied to broken skin. • This single-stemmed perennial produces seed-like fruits with tufts of white, hair-like bristles. **Where found:** open woods and slopes in submontane to subalpine zones.

Sitka Valerian

Valeriana sitchensis

Height: 1–3½ ft
Leaves: to 10 in long, in pairs on the stem, each divided into 3–7 leaflets
Flowers: ⅛–¼ in long, white to pale pink
Fruit: egg-shaped, ribbed achenes, ⅛–¼ in long

If the delicate flower clusters of this plant don't catch your attention, the odor may. Dried, frozen or bruised plants have a strong, unpleasant smell. • The stems are 4-sided, and the seed-like fruits are tipped with feathery hairs. • This perennial was widely used as a sedative. The tranquilizer and muscle relaxant diazepam (Valium) was first extracted from valerian. **Where found:** moist to wet sites in foothills to subalpine zones; from northern Canada to Idaho and Montana.

Bracken Fern

Pteridium aquilinum

Height: fronds to 10 ft or taller
Leaves: blades triangular, 10 or more leaflets

This widespread species is common around the world and occurs in a wide variety of habitats, though in our area, it prefers open or disturbed sites. • The deep rhizomes spread easily and help the plant to survive fires. • Native groups used the fronds to line pit ovens and ate the rhizomes. **Where found:** meadows, disturbed sites, clearings; dry to wet forests, lakeshores, bogs; low to subalpine elevations.

Sword Fern

Polystichum munitum

Height: up to 5 ft
Leaves: blades lance-shaped, numerous leaflets

Plants in the genus *Polystichum* are all large, tufted, evergreen ferns that form crown-like bunches from a single woody rhizome. The sword fern is one of several *Polystichum* species in our area. • This plant was used by Native groups for lining pit ovens, wrapping and storing food, flooring and bedding. • These ferns have large, circular sori (groups of spore sacs on the undersides of the leaflets). **Where found:** moist forests; low to mid elevations.

Maidenhair Fern

Adiantum pedatum

Height: 6–24 in
Leaves: palmate, numerous leaflets

Though it grows in colonies and can appear lush, this delicate fern typically has a single or very few palmately branched leaves on thin, dark brown or purple-black stems. • This fern was often used in Native basketry as well as medicinally. It was exported to Europe and used in herbal cough medicines. **Where found:** shady, humus-rich sites; forests, alongside streams and waterfalls; low to mid elevations. **Also known as:** *A. aleuticum.*

Surf Grass

Phyllospadix spp.

Length: 3 ft

Not algae, not grass, but a type of flowering plant, surf grass is the only flowering plant that is truly marine. It spends almost its entire life underwater, rarely exposed at low tide, when long, narrow, bright green strands can be seen in shallow, rocky waters. • Sea grass flowers are tiny and inconspicuous because there is no need to attract insects for pollination. Pollen is released in long, thread-like strands and carried by water currents. The seeds are dispersed by water or fish. **Where found:** rocky coasts exposed to wave action.

Turkish Towel · Red Algae

Gigartina exasperata

Length: up to 6 ft

Most marine plants are algae—lacking flowers, leaves or roots. There are 3 types of algae along California's coast: green, brown and red. Turkish towel is among the most massive of red algae species. Red algae are the largest group of seaweeds. They are the most abundant and comprise most species of seaweed in the world. Two of the most notable along the California coast include nori (*Porphyra* spp., cultivated in East Asia and routinely used in Japanese cooking) and Turkish towel. • A red pigment typically masks the chlorophyll that would otherwise render these algae green in color. **Where found:** intertidal and low, subtidal zones.

Giant Kelp · Brown Algae

Macrocystis spp.

Length: up to 330 ft

Macrocystis pyrifera is the most admired brown algae and is the foundation for the entire marine ecosystem. It is particularly suited to the cold Pacific waters. • Giant kelp is the largest and fastest growing plant in the marine environment. The entire frond is able to photosynthesize and, under ideal conditions, this plant is able to grow up to 2 ft in a single day. • Kelp forests are among the most biodiverse forests, including terrestrial ones, in the world. **Where found:** in waters 50–68°F, on rocky substrate where the plant can attach.

Giant Kelp · Brown Algae

Macrocystis spp.

Length: up to 330 ft

Macrocystis pyrifera is the most admired brown algae and is the foundation for the entire marine ecosystem. It is particularly suited to the cold Pacific waters. • Giant kelp is the largest and fastest growing plant in the marine environment. The entire frond is able to photosynthesize and, under ideal conditions, this plant is able to grow up to 2 ft in a single day. • Kelp forests are among the most biodiverse forests, including terrestrial ones, in the world. **Where found:** in waters 50–68°F, on rocky substrate where the plant can attach.

Bull Kelp · Brown Algae

Nereocystis luetkeana

Length: 30–60 ft; up to 115 ft

Bull kelp forests provide habitat and shelter for a myriad of marine life—sea otters wrap themselves up in bull kelp that is adhered to the ocean floor so that they can take a nap without drifting away. • Bull kelp is hollow with a bulbous float at the top and is filled with gasses that are 10% carbon monoxide. **Where found:** attached to rocky substrates; populations are increasingly abundant north of San Francisco Bay.

Sea Lettuce · Green Algae

Ulva lactuca

Length: 7 in

There are few green algae species found in the intertidal zone, but the most visible and abundant is the bright green sea lettuce, which either attaches to rocks or is free-floating. • This algae has a very simple structure that is only 2 cells thick. • Sea lettuce has a high caloric value and is eaten by crabs and mollusks. **Where found:** shallow bays, lagoons, harbors and marshes; on rocks and other algae in intertidal and high-tide zones.

GLOSSARY

A

achene: a seed-like fruit, e.g., sunflower seed

alcids: a family of birds that includes puffins, murrelets, auklets and other similar birds

algae: simple photosynthetic aquatic plants lacking true stems, roots, leaves and flowers, and ranging in size from single-celled forms to giant kelp

altricial: animals that are helpless at birth or hatching

ammocetes: larval lamprey

anadromous: fish that migrate from salt water to fresh water to spawn

annual: plants that live for only 1 year or growing season

anterior: situated at or toward the front

aquatic: water frequenting

arboreal: tree frequenting

autotrophic: an organism that produces its own food, e.g., by photosynthesis

B

barbels: fleshy, whisker-like appendages found on some fish

basal leaf: a leaf arising from the base of a plant

benthic: bottom feeding

berry: a fleshy fruit, usually with several to many seeds

bivalve: a group of mollusks in which the animal is enclosed by 2 valves (shells)

bract: a leaf-like structure arising from the base of a flower or inflorescence

bracteole: a small bract borne on a leaf stalk

brood parasite: a bird that parasitizes other bird's nests by laying its eggs and then abandoning them for the parasitized birds to raise, e.g., brown-headed cowbird

bulb: a fleshy underground organ with overlapping, swollen scales, e.g., an onion

C

calyx: a collective term for the sepals of a flower

cambium: inner layers of tissue that transport nutrients up and down the plant stalk or trunk

canopy: the fairly continuous cover provided by the branches and leaves of adjacent trees

capsules: a dry fruit that splits open to release seeds

carapace: a protective bony shell (e.g., of a turtle) or exoskeleton (e.g., of beetles)

carnivorous: feeding primarily on meat

carrion: decomposing animal matter or carcass

catkin: a spike of small flowers

chelipeds: the clawed first pair of legs, e.g., on a crab

compound leaf: a leaf separated into 2 or more divisions called leaflets

cone: the fruit produced by a coniferous plant, composed of overlapping scales around a central axis

coniferous: cone-bearing; seed (female) and pollen (male) cones are borne on the same tree in different locations

corm: a swollen underground stem base used by some plants as an organ of propagation; resembles a bulb

crepuscular: active primarily at dusk and dawn

cryptic coloration: a coloration pattern designed to conceal an animal

D

deciduous: a tree whose leaves turn color and are shed annually

defoliating: dropping of the leaves

disk flower: a small flower in the center, or disk, of a composite flower
(e.g., aster, daisy or sunflower)
diurnal: active primarily during the day
dorsal: the top or back
drupe: a fleshy fruit with a stony pit, e.g., peach, cherry

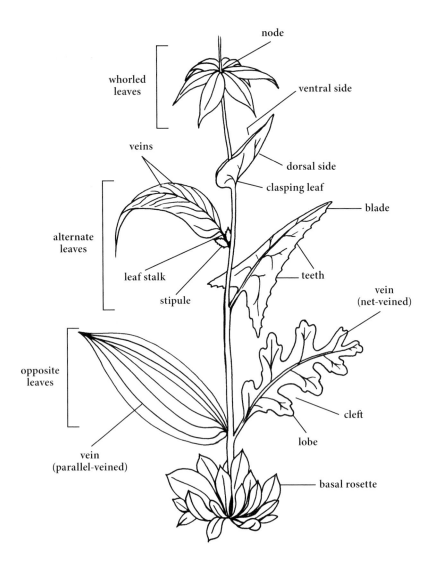

E

echolocation: navigation by rebounding sound waves off objects to target or avoid them

ecological niche: an ecological role filled by a species

ecoregion: distinction between regions based upon geology, climate, biodiversity, elevation and soil composition

ectoparasites: skin parasites

ectotherm: an animal that regulates its body temperature behaviorally from external sources of heat, i.e., from the sun

eft: the stage of a newt's life following the tadpole stage, in which it exits the water and leads a terrestrial life; when the newt matures to adulthood it returns to the water

endotherm: an animal that regulates its body temperature internally

estivate: a state of inactivity and a slowing of the metabolism to permit survival in extended periods of high temperatures and inadequate water supply

estuarine: an area where a freshwater river exits into the sea; the salinity of the seawater drops because it is diluted by the fresh water

eutrophic: a nutrient-rich body of water with an abundance of algae growth and a low level of dissolved oxygen

evergreen: having green leaves through winter; not deciduous

exoskeleton: a hard outer encasement that provides protection and points of attachment for muscles

F

flight membrane: the membrane between the fore and hind limbs of bats and some squirrels that allows bats to fly and squirrels to glide through the air

follicle: the structure in the skin from which hair or feathers grow; a dry fruit that splits open along a single line on one side when ripe; a cocoon

food web: the elaborated, interconnected feeding relationships of living organisms in an ecosystem

forb: a broad-leaved plant that lacks a permanent woody stem and loses its aboveground growth each year; may be annual, biennial or perennial

G

gillrakers: long, thin, fleshy projections that protect delicate gill tissue from particles in the water

glandular: similar to or containing glands

H

habitat: the physical area in which an organism lives

hawking: feeding behavior in which a bird leaves a perch, snatches its prey in mid-air, and then returns to its previous perch

herbaceous: feeding primarily on vegetation

hibernation: a state of decreased metabolism and body temperature and slowed heart and respiratory rates to permit survival during long periods of cold temperature and diminished food supply

hibernaculum: a shelter in which an animal, usually a mammal, reptile or insect, chooses to hibernate

hind: female elk (this term is used mostly in Asia—in North America "cow" is more often used)

hips: the berry-like fruit of some plants in the rose family (Rosaceae)

holdfast: the root-like structure that seaweeds use to hold onto rocky substrates

hybrids: the offspring from a cross between parents belonging to different varieties or subspecies, sometimes between different subspecies or genera

I

incubate: to keep eggs at a relatively constant temperature until they hatch

inflorescence: a cluster of flowers on a stalk; may be arranged as a spike, raceme, head, panicle, etc.

insectivorous: feeding primarily on insects

intertidal zone: the area between low- and high-tide lines

invertebrate: any animal lacking a backbone, e.g., worms, slugs, crayfish, shrimps

involucral bract: one of several bracts that form a whorl below a flower or flower cluster

K

key: a winged fruit, usually of an ash or maple; also called a "samara"

L

larva: immature forms of an animal that differ from the adult

leaflet: a division of a compound leaf

lenticel: a slightly raised portion of bark where the cells are packed more loosely, allowing for gas exchange with the atmosphere

lobate: having each toe individually webbed

lobe: a projecting part of a leaf or flower, usually rounded

M

metabolic rate: the rate of chemical processes in an organism

metamorphosis: the developmental transformation of an animal from larval to sexually mature adult stage

midden: the pile of cone scales found on the territories of tree squirrels, usually under a favorite tree

molt: when an animal sheds old feathers, fur or skin, in order to replace them with new growth

montane: of mountainous regions

myccorhizal fungi: fungi that has a mutually beneficial relationship with the roots of some seed plants

N

neotropical migrant: a bird that nests in North America, but overwinters in the New World tropics

nocturnal: active primarily at night

node: a slightly enlarged section of a stem where leaves or branches originate

nudibranch: sea slug

nutlet: a small, hard, single-seeded fruit that remains closed

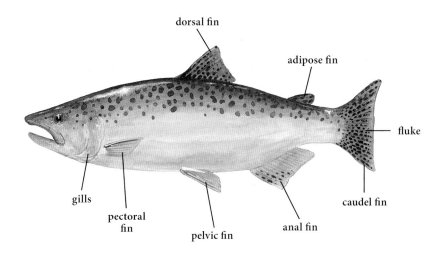

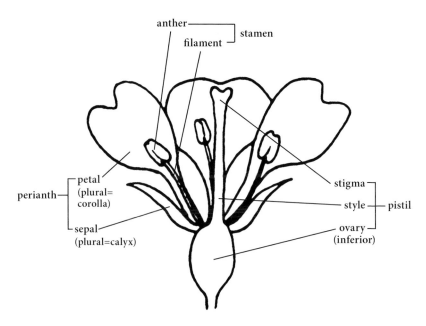

O

omnivorous: feeding on both plants and animals

ovoid: egg-shaped

P

palmate: leaflets, lobes or veins arranged around a single point, like the fingers on a hand (e.g., maple leaf)

pappus: the modified calyx of composite flowers (e.g., asters or daisies), consisting of awns, scales or bristles at the apex of the achene

parasite: a relationship between 2 species in which one benefits at the expense of the other

patagium: skin forming a flight membrane

pelage: the fur or hair of mammals

perennial: a plant that lives for several years

petal: a member of the inside ring of modified flower leaves, usually brightly colored or white

phenology: stages of growth as influenced by climate

photosynthesis: conversion of CO_2 and water into sugars via energy of the sun

pinniped: a marine mammal with limbs that are modified to form flippers; a seal, sea-lion or walrus

pioneer species: a plant species that is capable of colonizing an otherwise unvegetated area; one of the first species to take hold in a disturbed area

piscivorous: fish-eating

pishing: a noise made to attract birds

pistil: the female organ of a flower, usually consisting of an ovary, style and stigma

plastic species: a species that can adapt to a wide range of conditions

plastron: the lower part of a turtle or tortoise shell, which covers the abdomen

poikilothermic: having a body temperature that is the same as the external environment and varies with it

pollen: the tiny grains produced in a plant's anthers and which contain the male reproductive cells

pollen cone: male cone that produces pollen

polyandry: a mating strategy in which one female mates with several males

pome: a fruit with a core, e.g., apple

precocial: animals who are active and independent at birth or hatching

prehensile: able to grasp

proboscis: the elongated tubular and flexible mouthpart of many insects

R

ray flower: in a composite flower (e.g., aster, daisy or sunflower), a type of flower usually with long, colorful petals that collectively make up the outer ring of petals (the center of a composite flower is composed of disk flowers)

redd: spawing nest for fish

resinous: bearing resin, usually causing stickiness

rhinopores: tentacle-like sensory structures on the head of a nudibranch (sea slug)

rhizome: a horizontal underground stem

rictal bristles: hair-like feathers found on the faces of some birds

riparian: on the bank of a river or other watercourse

rookery: a colony of nests

runner: a slender stolon or prostrate stem that roots at the nodes or the tip

S

samara: a dry, winged fruit with usually only a single seed (e.g., maple or ash); also called a "key"

salmonid: a member of the Salmonidae family of fishes; includes trout, char, salmon, whitefish and grayling

scutes: individual plates on a turtle's shell

seed cone: female cone that produces seeds

sepal: the outer, usually green, leaf-like structures that protect the flower bud and are located at the base of an open flower

silicle: a fruit of the mustard family (Brassicaceae) that is 2-celled and usually short, wide and often flat

silique: a long, thin fruit with many seeds; characteristic of some members of the mustard family (Brassicaceae)

sorus (pl. sori): a collection of sporangia under a fern frond; in some lichens and fungi, a structure that produces pores

spadix: a fleshy spike with many small flowers

spathe: a leaf-like sheath that surrounds a spadix

spur: a pointed projection

stamen: the pollen-bearing organ of a flower

stigma: a receptive tip in a flower that receives pollen

stolon: a long branch or stem that runs along the ground and often propagates more plants

subnivean: below the surface of the snow

substrate: the surface that an organism grows on; the material that makes up a streambed (e.g., sand or gravel)

suckering: a method of tree and shrub reproduction in which shoots arise from an underground stem

syrinx: a bird's vocal organ

T

taproot: the main, large root of a plant from which smaller roots arise, e.g., carrot

tendril: a slender, clasping or twining outgrowth from a stem or a leaf

terrestrial: land frequenting

torpor: a state of physical inactivity

tragus: a prominent structure of the outer ear of a bat

tubercule: a round nodule or warty outgrowth

tubular flower: a type of flower in which all or some of the petals are fused together at the base

tundra: a high-altitude ecological zone at the northernmost limits of plant growth, where plants are reduced to shrubby or mat-like growth

tympanum: eardrum; the hearing organ of a frog

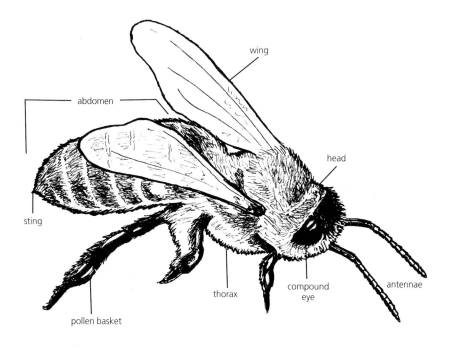

U

ungulate: an animal that has hooves

V

ventral: of or on the abdomen (belly)

vermiculations: wavy-patterned makings

vertebrate: an animal possessing a backbone

vibrissae: bristle-like feathers growing around the beak of birds to aid in catching insects

W

whorl: a circle of leaves or flowers around a stem

woolly: bearing long or matted hairs

REFERENCES

Acorn, John, and Ian Sheldon. 2002. *Bugs of Northern California.* Lone Pine Publishing, Edmonton, AB.

Bailey, Robert G. 1995. 2nd edition. *Descriptions of the Ecoregions of the United States.* United States Department of Agriculture Forest Service, Washington, D.C. http://www.fs.fed.us/rm/analytics/publications/ecoregionsindex.html. Accessed July 2007.

Bailey, Robert G. 1995. 2nd edition. *Descriptions of the Ecoregions of the United States.* United States Department of Agriculture Forest Service, Washington, D.C. http://www.fs.fed.us/rm/analytics/staff/Bailey.html. Accessed July 2007.

Bezener, Andy, and Linda Kershaw. 1999. *Rocky Mountain Nature Guide.* Lone Pine Publishing, Edmonton, AB.

Blackwell, Laird R. 1997. *Wildflowers of the Tahoe Sierra.* Lone Pine Publishing, Edmonton, AB.

Blackwell, Laird R. 1999. *Wildflowers of the Sierra Nevada and the Central Valley.* Lone Pine Publishing, Edmonton, AB.

California State Parks. California Department of Parks and Recreation. http://www.parks.ca.gov/?page_id=21491. Accessed December 2007.

Complete List of Amphibians, Reptile, Bird and Mammal Species in California. California Department of Fish and Game. http://www.dfg.ca.gov/bdb/pdfs/species_list.pdf. Accessed March 2006.

Eder, Tamara. 2002. *Whales and other Marine Mammals of California and Baja.* Lone Pine Publishing, Edmonton, AB.

Eder, Tamara. 2005. *Mammals of California.* Lone Pine Publishing, Edmonton, AB.

Fix, David, and Andy Bezener. 2000. *Birds of Northern California.* Lone Pine Publishing, Edmonton, AB.

Jepson, Willis Linn. 1909. *Trees of California.* Cunningham, Curtis and Welch, San Francisco.

Leatherwood, Stephen, and Randall R. Reeves. 1983. *The Sierra Club Handbook of Whales and Dolphins.* Sierra Club Books, San Francisco.

National Audubon Society. 1998. *Field Guide to North American Fishes, Whales and Dolphins.* Chanticleer Press, Toronto, ON.

National Audubon Society. 1998. *Field Guide to North American Seashore Creatures*. Chanticleer Press, Toronto, ON.

National Parks: California. U.S. Department of the Interior. http://www.nps.gov/state/ca/. Accessed December 2007.

Sheldon, Ian. 1998. *Animal Tracks of Northern California*. Lone Pine Publishing, Edmonton, AB.

Sheldon, Ian. 1999. *Seashore of Northern and Central California*. Lone Pine Publishing, Edmonton, AB.

Snyderman, Marty. 1998. *California Marine Life: A Guide to Common Marine Species*. Roberts Rinehart, Niwot, CO.

St. John, Alan. 2002. *Reptiles of the Northwest: California to Alaska, Rockies to the Coast*. Lone Pine Publishing, Edmonton, AB.

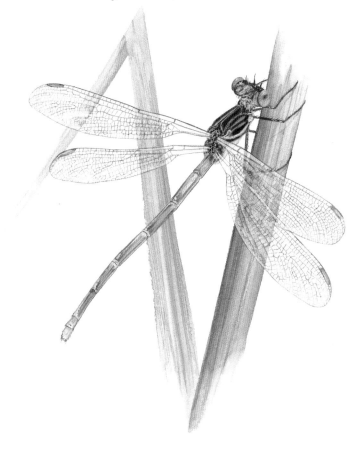

INDEX

Names in **boldface** type indicate primary species.

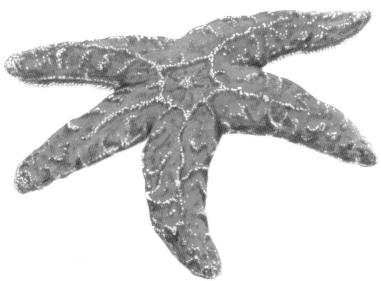

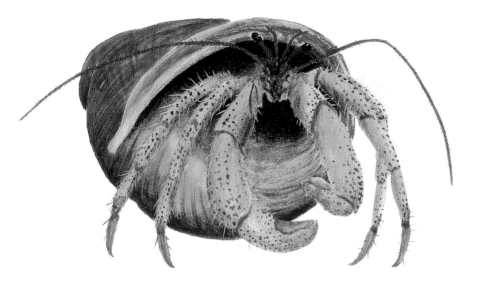

ABOUT THE AUTHOR

Erin McCloskey spent her formative years observing nature from atop her horse. She received her BSc with distinction in environmental and conservation sciences, majoring in conservation biology and management. An active campaigner for the protection of endangered species and spaces, Erin has collaborated with various NGOs and has been involved in numerous conservation projects around the world. Currently, she is the North American operations manager for Biosphere Expeditions, located in Los Angeles. Erin began working as an editor with Lone Pine Publishing in 1996. From 2000–05, she lived in Italy, where she freelanced as a writer and editor; she was managing editor for *AK: Journal of Applied Kinesiology* and helped prepare scientific articles for several medical research institutions. She also worked as an editor for several publishers focused on nature and travel. Erin is the author of *The Bradt Travel Guide to Argentina, Ireland Flying High, Canada Flying High, Hawaii From the Air* and co-author for the *Green Volunteers* guidebook series. She is also the author of the *Washington and Oregon Nature Guide* for Lone Pine Publishing.